The Suspect We

Roxanna Bennett
Shane Neilson

Palimpsest Press
1171 Eastlawn Ave.
Windsor, Ontario. N8S 3J1
www.palimpsestpress.ca

Printed and bound in Canada
Cover design and book typography by Ellie Hastings
Edited by Jim Johnstone

Palimpsest Press would like to thank the Canada Council for the Arts and the Ontario Arts Council for their support of our publishing program. We also acknowledge the assistance of the Government of Ontario through the Ontario Book Publishing Tax Credit.

ONTARIO ARTS COUNCIL
CONSEIL DES ARTS DE L'ONTARIO
an Ontario government agency
un organisme du gouvernement de l'Ontario

Canada Council   Conseil des Arts
for the Arts   du Canada

ONTARIO | ONTARIO
CREATES | CRÉATIF

Canada

LIBRARY AND ARCHIVES CANADA CATALOGUING IN PUBLICATION

TITLE: The suspect we / Roxanna Bennett, Shane Neilson.
NAMES: Bennett, Roxanna, 1971- author. | Neilson, Shane, 1975- author.
IDENTIFIERS: Canadiana (print) 20230150888
            Canadiana (ebook) 2023015090X

ISBN 9781990293405 (SOFTCOVER)
ISBN 9781990293412 (EPUB)
CLASSIFICATION: LCC PS8603.E55955 S87 2023 | DDC C811/.6—DC23

The Suspect We

May you be free of suffering.
May we be free of suspicion.

Roxanna Bennett

Shane Neilson

CONTENTS

And they both sat there, grown up, yet children at heart; and it was summer,
– warm, beautiful summer

— Hans Christian Andersen

An only life can take so long to climb
Clear of its wrong beginnings, and may never

— Philip Larkin

BOOK 1:
Subject to Question

Otherine

For those who doubt, then this coordinated pharmacopeia:
a Maritimes of small drugs and baby steps, sertraline
of South Street in Halifax, venlafaxine of University Street
in Saint John, then olanzapine's palace of high windows
and gunmetal blue makeup – the jump zone. An Ontario
for escalation: condo row house on Rhonda Road in Guelph,
suburbish, but with communal pool; the drug's whisper,
what was it? A sibilant -*ine* after the staccato consonants.
O yes, oxycarbemazapine, leading a parade of other -*ines*
to come. Lithium for Powell St. South's postwar construction,
its tenement brick a stolid salute to phlegmatic health,
soot-scorched if you knew where to look. As if storms
had antidotes, clonazepam marshalled for unpredictable sky –
the worst kind, baby blue. Then a series of temporized *buts*
from a backyard and bedroom empire you can never feel: but
valproic acid, but aripiprazole, but lurasidone.   But
they hear suffixed nouns as a form of belief?   But
I have the dry heaves of authenticity. But. A body.   But
a body in motion can be quelled. But balance?   But
freedom? But nighttime. But they take my words!   But
I only want to die. Take with food: *no ifs, ands, or buts.*
But outside my window, every night of my life, past
the dull face staring back, is a focal point of the water tower,
that height of –*ine:* less cure or solution but etymological
metaphor (yes, I daily dose the *OED*): "Forming adjectives,
representing Latin -*īnus*, -*īna*, -*īnum*, added to names
of persons, animals, or material things, and to some other
words, with the sense 'of' or 'pertaining to', 'of the nature of'."
They claim the tower isn't a drug? But I took it like that,
each night; anyway, prayers and drugs are indistinguishable.
Pertaining to love, a differently drugged me might write,
"But what other word do audiences want? What do they need?"
They have answers that begin with *But.* I rebut: the drugs
were metallic wafers on my tongue, proof I was reviled market,

suspect truth, risk to self and others, and doing the right thing,
but in lieu. By lack. For and of the sad consolations. Here
in Oakville, on a queen-size, I consent to capsule the circle
and pestle this poem into drug. I say lamotrigine to the duvet,
its powder-taste summoned to serve as dispassionate drug
passport, less subject in the kingdom of the ill than subject
to question. F-ine. Yes,
I am in love, *of; pertaining to; of the nature of,* singing *-ine.*

♥. Formative Elements

Thalidomide for mothers
cocaine in Coca-cola

saltpeter in the rations
smallpox for the Others

caffeine for the workers
sugar for the slackers

formative habits
are chemically coloured

Dark red deworming liquid
orange Triaminic   chalky pink

calamine lotion   snot-thick
yellow penicillin   vitamins

rainbowing spit-out castor
& iron pills   King-sized

Rothman's in the royal
blue package   dark brown

tobacco in sticky loose shreds
stiff oily smears on

child-sized pajamas
glucose cortisol adrenaline

❦ I drank every day for ten years to help with the shame

When drunk, I'd stare in the bathroom mirror
and wonder: *Why are you here?* Shame stared
back: *Go away, unwanted, go away, not of us,*

go away. As a child watching my father get drunk
I'd pull the blanket to my head as reflecting
darkness. *Never look at your face again. Blank's*

not you. I'm you. Love should have worked, but love,
in its ruined form, would have to be for later. I,
on quests to pass as human, wanted to be real,

sailing in a ship called my body, sculpted in the image
of recidivist gods, unseen in invisible registers
yet recognized as *different* to the human witnesses,

as altered flesh-bag of unbridgeable synapse,
with glia too inertial and postures too strange
for a mold, and in my wake this chorus: *Does he know?*

Does he even know he's not normal? Blessed
to never be Narcissus, I hated my face, banishing it
until each drunken night's shame declension.

O, sensorium flaw: my face cannot signal the soul
or properly worship humans in reproduction
of their vanity. All I have are words to create

a foolish myth about a spectrum of shame
some bear, like occult fire, a radiation that needs
the gear of mirrors to find authentication.

I'm not here! Not like you! Scales and questionnaries
so determine, and no mirror session ever uncovered
my hidden impulses. Just a duller null. These words,

I could speak them to the face in the mirror;
they are in love, but a love told to *go away, go away,*
to self-extinguish, told in turn by a body that agreed

to turn as told. I can't come back, not with no face
in humanland. These words – they are in love,
but not as powerful as the normality of the gods.

🥀. I spent a year drunk to help with the shame

but my body's not able to sustain
that much poison. Still, I avoid
the bathroom mirror, too weak to gaze

back at the family face in the glass,
Why am I still here? As a kid
when the grown-ups got drunk, I braced

for broken glass, splintering darkness
saying I was *unwanted, unlikable,
unloveable. Nowhere is safe,*

Go away, go away, I prayed.
If myths aren't enough
to save souls how am I still here?

Incarnating in my imperfect form
the mother of all myths: *Abnormal.*
I was the Fool, I believed the gods

condemned me, that I was strange,
sculpted from no usual stuff, unseen
by visible registers yet recognized

as *different,* as alien – with postures
too strange for a mold,
Does she know? Does she even know –

lesser, never to be, *not like us.* We feel it.
I want to love the face in the mirror.
What proof exists that all beings accept?

💐 Radiation Burns

On quests to pass as human
I worked   married   went to therapy

wanted to be a real person
like the ones on TV

friends   social outings   hobbies
intimacy

I practised making faces to greet
the faces that I met hating

the face that failed me
& its mystery

In the mirror
I rehearsed conversations

never missed an appointment
or a deadline

until inevitably –
Radiation burns

I need

no authentication
unflawed sensorium

the tower is inhuman
pain & love

The quest

I need no authentication
pain supplies all I need.

As a child, the human-detector
despaired of finding me.

Hey, over there, a stone
amidst an empire of glass.

I once tried to burn a stone,
to bring it inside my body;

the stone was kind, said –
I do not burn.

A body at rest
tends to stay at rest.

Even better than
even better than

even better than
the real thing.

Over here, over there,
turn over every stone.

A stillness undergirds
the glass empire.

The stillness doesn't move.
The stillness

doesn't move.
The quest is redefined.

Who Projects What Project?

Last month, I submitted an article about autism to a medical journal, asking the obvious question: with so many specialties perfect for doctors without "social skills," and with medicine perfect for "rigid people with good memories," then why isn't there data about people with autism in the profession?

The answer I got back: "Maybe if you wrote a different article about the creeping medicalization of normative life, that would be perfect." Also: "I prefer to think about people with abilities, with strengths. Like you, for example. You have a freakish ability with words."

Less

Am I more shame
than human

or is it human
to feel such shame?

Being human,
I'm afraid

I've forgotten
everything

but shades
of antipsychotic blue

Validated Inventories

Each question of the suspect we:

Have you thought –

Have you thought –

Have you thought –

Itinerary, inventory, have *you* thought
about jumping from a promontory?

I have, I have thought –

Single symptom known as goodbye –
and I, suicide, suicide I? Decades

of degree, collective we,

you can catch in my face a blur, not a blank,
or a book of unwritten cheques

for all the checks and balances

of the safety republics,
Officer Default Restraint.

Fuck you too, Officer Escalation Clause.

I, just dumb bludgeoned love

by a truncheon, a repose posture the doctors
call waxy flexibility, but rigid soul.

What are you waiting for?

asks the mirror. Behind it, the medicine cabinet
is stuffed full of wait, old drugs

that archive all the beautiful,

failed attempts to prolong wait. Wait – who am
I confessing to? Mirror, paper, or the mirthful sky?

To the usual audience

who would have the record otherwise,
the ledger of love is kept in the black.

I have thought not of flock, but of flight,

of all symptoms lifting off in the night
and roosting in the water tower,

squabbling about score traded

for velocity, sharing this *Wisdom* as salve:
we wait for what may not come,

we wait for what we do

not question the wait for what, we do
not question if we have thought,

for we have thought, and thought again.

🏵 Invalid Inventories of the Chronically Traumatized

Yes, every bridge I've crossed has been derelict,
I've stockpiled Clonazepam & can tell you
where the razors are, the bleach, the kerosene,
no jokes about the oven, please,
I always thought going to sleep with the car running
was the nicest, or a hot bath with a long blade,
so quiet, but messy, inconsiderate, like lying
down in traffic   Calculate
the eternal equation, waiting versus
the unbearable pain of being *not us*
the needlepointed constellation invisibly
registered   indelibly rendered in sinew
Where's the proof   Forged   re-forget terribly
reminded   Terribly mind the interrogative

🌾 Not us is an able bodied given

Not us is an able bodied given,
the "starting gate position"
traumatologists deem. Ask lovers

if they are in love, and the ones
that are do not cite act and deed
but rather the simple ease

of being beside. As in, manifest
the invisible thing. As in, do you
hear the song, or do you feel it

in your body? You, too, have a body.
The love between bodies
cannot be proven except in the way

Thomas touched Jesus's flank.
Oh, and I don't mean
"love as wound." I mean here I am,

despised, and already dead,
still singing, singing still,
of stillness. How many verifications

until I die, symptom checkpoints
of ideal form? Not a proof,
but a passionate declaration

which, if you've ever heard
a certain kind of song, should
be above suspicion, below

a stone.

♣ We do not question if we have thought, for we have thought, & thought again

& again, neural pathways worn through
by the ruthless loop
of *please go away stop don't go*

the deeper pattern inlaid in
the grey matter   runes in the grooves

you are worthless helpless hopeless
a piece of shit & everybody knows this
Why don't you fucking die

reinforced at every appointment
by indifference & nihilism

& now I question the accretion of prejudice
on a foundation of misunderstanding
what a bodymind even is

according to what passes for medicine
it is not what my senses detect

I question every thought:
is it true, can I prove it, if you turn it inside out
no one lives in this bodymind

but me & ghosts & I am   trying   to choose
to believe   I am free

The Abled Nuclear Romance

I do not ask permission to tell.
We're long past that. Long ago,

I tried to share the difficulty
to generic publics and was told:

But you're still his father!
and *"He can still have a happy life!"*

Well, yes? Over and over, I tried to make
them understand, but they couldn't,

or wouldn't. You see the sameness
in this secret traffic? I choose to say

couldn't from long experience
with the greatest of teachers, my son,

who is made of a resistant patience.
Oh? Offensive? Abuse? That's

your neck of the woods to patrol.

*

I see the appeal of the dream:
proud dad teaches son tasks,

responsibility, data about the world.
How nice. We're voice-to-text

here, but only the computer seems
to listen, and imperfectly.

Ignored warnings, too close
to bodies, no sense of time,

relationships as immediate abacuses
of now – when we come walking

along our street, others go in
their houses and hide. And we understand,

it's where Abled Nuclear Romance
lives, perpetually unwitnessed

and thereby unverified to live forever.
Agency in the world? Travel?

Speech being heard, of future
fact after future fact – me, at eight years old:

I'll leave here and be in love.

*

In the background, a clamoring
I've heard in public and private

when saying a simple truth.   .
Reader, I hear the protest rising

in your bodymind – am I allowed
to speak with such testimony?

No one can say he was not loved
or protected from everyone

and everything, institutions second-
most, and himself the chief.

Though they would say. This they say
whenever I tell the truth.

In the pandemic, we slowly die.
The toddler has learned to scream

to make him go away from a wife
who is not loved by him

and who does not love him back –
such innings, my friends, long days

that I can say I understand. Can you?
Are you still listening? – and me,

always in lieu, master of lack,
who greets him with a smile

in the morning. Small proof, but I need
show nothing to this world other

than the prejudice plain on its face.
I hold Stendhal's mirror.

Come and see the love, if you would,
in action. Be unlike the neighbors

on our street, I welcome you to be his friend.
By this interested act, you would be

his one friend. Still, a dull love
on meeting, ineradicable – all the vended

stories of oppression, of system, from tone
to inflection, yet my son – we must not speak

the name of the Abled Nuclear Romance?

♥. The Unenabled Queer Dream

I hate parades & attention
so never think to mention

& besides, Steve's a cishetdude –
it's rude to assume anything

about anyone except
that each person is a person,

worthy & deserving & each being
has a reason for being & I don't need

permission to be or to love them
(no one does, listen, listen)

narrative is the only power &
medicine – it's a trap, parameters

set in haphazard arrogance,
one stupid assumption after another

makes a tower designed to collapse
at the first sign of strangeness

or biological facts machines
can't measure yet, it's enough to drive

one or billions Mad, insanity
is denying the evidence of the senses

or the thousands of years of healing
recorded before we got here

with our bright ideas, is it possible
western science is a little bit biased,

dividing bodyminds into tinier
& tinier compartments & separating

each section from the living
heedless of its function

in the larger system, almost like
oh, I don't know an action

could cause an equal & opposite
reaction? I don't know, I'm no scientist,

cut me up, no problem, never mind
that Einstein said relativity

was a local phenomenon
or that neuroscience takes notes

when the Dalai Lama speaks, nope,
saw me up, I'm just meat,

& if it breathes & eats, get to work,
that's all you're worth,

just another body ground up
in the big machine, & the doctors

can't know better, they're conditioned
to be "smarter" & are gifted

by our culture authority to cast
anyone they like to the vultures

"My hands are tied" is another
way of saying, *You're not worth*

my attention, I hope you die

*

Fuck university & all the programmed
fantasies of a "normal life"

a job some kids a mortgage & a wife
I say this having lusted after normalcy

& its trappings of legitimacy
all my life, failing in the ways we

measure each other's worth:
career, money, objects, "achievements,"

likes & favourites, praise & prizes,
friends & titles & labels like straight

& sane & nice. Happy is a hard-won
skill that makes space for the pain

not a list of things to tell us apart
or a pardon, more like an unguarded well

of love anyone can draw from
I feel your scorn & raise you

since I've been where you're from
& I wouldn't, didn't, couldn't listen either,

was unable, was as close-minded
as a doctor who can't conceive

of other reasons or see their own
conditioning colouring

their decisions & revisions

*

I feel the protest rising in your bodymind
I feel that same rigidity in mine

made up of problems & patterns
& assumptions & battering

gridlock in the ganglia

None may allow or forbid & yet
I ask often if I can, bristle

at shadows, change, rebuff
but would like to befriend

& free myself enough
to not stop fumbling for love

By the CanLit Dumpster Fire, I Sat Down and Wept

The performativity of the physical act:
by the selfie stick, I sat down and wept –
by the big blue garbage bin, I sat down and wept –
by the CanLit dumpster fire, I sat down and wept –
by the scaffolded Christ in St. Vincent de Paul Church,
I sat down and wept.

Jesus wept,

trauma-informed care wept, patient-centred research
wept, and my poems, they wept too, truly; I sit
next to them and weep as they visit, proving I'm alive.
All buzzwords and good causes, they wept at the prospect
of consumption, for they were made to be consumed,
vended, and sat down next to themselves.

Fuck the conformity that says, "Poet, do the work."
Because, of course, no one sat next to me,
no one wept.

(And because the poems of others,
I don't want them to *cry*. I want them,
at least, to change the world, to give
me back the chance to stand.)

Would I have trusted the weepers, never sending
to know for whom the bell tolls? Who weeps
for the weepers?

No tears

confirmed I was alive then, so it's poetry that gives me
the capacity now to sit down next to myself and weep.

❦. Each Day I Sit in *Sukhasana* & Weep

I cry at least a little every day
& when I read your poems

      ignorance is bliss, administering
      performances a kind of sick

to cause such suffering, the lack
of care, the mirror's raging

      packaged as this era's saving
      sold back in bitter bite-sized

squares. Fuck conformity,
the fear of being weird & free

      & deprived of approval,
      love abides. I had to google

"Poet, do the work" but am unable
I sit, beside everyone & no one

      & it's pretty peaceful
      when you refuse to prove

(they aren't listening, can't understand
through the layers of conditioning)

      that you deserve to be alive.
      I weep & want to change

the world, to give myself
a chance to "stand"

      but the ground we've made
      is hateful, so hardened

Nekkhamma

In all its forms, normative: you, with a tempest
for a mind; you, with the flood; you and you,
you lack the discipline, training, and inclination to
be ethical in the world. *Fuck off*, in other words,
to all youse. Yet these words, wrested as a fraction
of the total in surplus from what is called consciousness
at a cross-section in time called the poem – oh, deluge –
serve as submerged signal, a swerving flotsam sense
clings to, as if to say, lest I'm thought unworthy
of life with the blankest face, *I am here*. I can't sit
still or stop moving; how to non-attach to motion
and emotion? On the run, this bodymind finds respite
from pain by not stopping, distraction as strategy
for dysregulation and alternative sensory apparatus.
(Who wrote the book of love for autistics, and
the book of pain? I'll take the survival guide first.)
Yes, world, pain catches up. Where, though,
might there be a word that suffices to work
a charm other than the rain, or my wife's
touch on my back? Then, with no thought or idea,
the threshold overwhelmed, I cannot think to ask
for a substitute. (If I did, I'd bring back a demon.)
So the world is too much with me, too;
we're acquaintances, deformed by the mutual
disinclination to address one another in recognition.
Cue white noise, cue all the garbage dumps,
cue all the lovers clinging to one another like ballast,
promising to never let go, and in the promise,
perhaps, a mutual disinclination to be stained by thought.

✿. "Work through your issues already!"

You, with a tempest for a mind;
you, the flood; you & you,
why can't I be as clear as you

to say what I mean
rarely seems kind

– oh, deluge –
cling to me
I'm unworthy

I am here.

I can't sit
still or stop moving;
how to non-attach to motion

& emotion?
Can pain be without world?
Am I a demon

formed
by inclination
to recognize

my pain in yours

◀ Gratitude for The Self Who Learned

Gratitude for fire; for resistance; for refusing the lie. For rest, and accepting the lie as not mine, never mine, also letting it be. For relations of body, such quelling crook of arm around a belly. For children who know what they want (I am awed by anyone who wants); for a specific river; for a table that knows more about life than people; for a Guelph sky that granted my wish on November 15, 2010; for words; for the price of things, the cost; for doubt and disdain; for pain; for Alden Nowlan's "He Sits Down on the Floor for the School of the Retarded" and the sudden intensity of each thwarted life; for how my hands, arms, and feet respond to touch; for the configuration of my father's face; for Lithium as sater of emotions I can't name; for the Book of Names; for grey strands in black hair; for a 15 hour drive home that's gone now; for my wife's calm; for a twenty dollar bill snuck by a girlfriend into a bottle of Scotch, her handwriting said she loved me; Bible word, righteous sting; cold husk of morning; infrequent rain on aluminum roofs; barns too close to waterfront; every high-placed righteous face that said, "I told you so"; how in a child's face, there is a different message; for a constitutional non-conformity; for standing, so much standing, in a metaphorical corner; for getting up from the dirt (has your mouth commingled blood and dirt?); for some half-dead crooner at the Grand Ole Opry belting out a greatest hit because we all needed it; for hearing every kind word and registering them too late, being bruised by the hate; the learning was here, now, that is the lesson, here, now

🐞 Gratitude for The Self Who Learned

like water is fire is air is earth is an ocean that's still old & new; gratitude for the self who learned things like how to open a bank account without ID or acquire food without money; gratitude for the self who learned how to drag a backpack full of cans from the food bank up four flights of stairs in a heat wave, how to breastfeed while bleeding; gratitude for the self who learned how to get full custody, to navigate the system, to work full-time, parent full-time while trying to find help; gratitude for the self who learned it's OK to not be OK; gratitude for the self who learned how heavy a sleeping child can be, how to take a kid to school every single day while "crazy"; gratitude for the self who learned school didn't matter, anyway; gratitude for the self who learned how to come to alone after another operation, what poor wound healing means, how to make friends with animals & pain; gratitude for the self who learned how to wait in an Emergency room, how to wait in a waiting room, how to wait in an examination room, how to wait to be seen; gratitude for the self who learned it's okay to mourn someone you hate, it's complicated; gratitude for the self who learned the inefficacy of Plan B, who learned how much an abortion costs; gratitude for the self who learned the meaninglessness of time to a specialist; gratitude for the self who learned the difference between sane & not sane is a lanyard & a security pass; gratitude for the self who learned how to give everything away

🐺. Chronically Crying Wolf

People use the word *celebrate* a lot –
I've yet to find out what it means.
I've seen it on TV with champagne
and confetti, people who seem happy.
Mostly people apologize to me
when I make announcements,
like pregnancy. I mean, not now,
obviously. No one speaks to me.
People hate The Boy Who Cried Wolf
& the person whose diagnosis
& symptoms keep changing.
I feel the doubt & disdain in my body-
mind & stayed home for years
before the quarantine. The whole world
is locked-in with me but I am still alone.

Lupine

The one constant: difference. Less prophecy than fact.
But at the world's differential: so many false names,
more than exist for pain (is there a false name for pain?
Approximation is painful misidentification) and more
than for the cognate, abuse. All the false things, they
are common commodities. *Idiot, retard, moron, shithead,*
gimp, Rain Man – all misses at registering this wolf.
(Do you believe the myth of the wolf in sheep's clothing?
The true story is that the sheep wear wolf's clothing,
and beautifully.)

The pros performed no better: major depression, generalized
anxiety disorder, agitated depression, personality disorder –
even after promontory's plunge, no improvement in accuracy –
making me ask the boy who cried wolf from my favourite myth
of childhood

      let the approximation of thunder sound,
      let my father appear as reckoning and reckoner,
      let the world be spectator:

Boy, were you crying wolf to the world, demanding its clothing
in return for your lesson? Without friends or inclination, a face
that's blank but bears anger as default warning, and a passion
for the rainsound, *a freakish ability with words.* Where
are the sheep in this world, and how do we find the flock?

Suffering, a love letter

Jab the heart with the blame finger.
Look at sky, and suck all of the blue –
that delusional, child-killing blue,
yes, as you bring it in, you will inhale
furies and the body will metabolize
what some call pain but you call
pedagogy. At uncommon moments,
you will do the right things. Protection,
defense, even the terrible work
of fighting – and see how this work
is sameness.
                    For, with the internal blue,
blame now repurposed as sadness,
you'll find no new ideology or system
can alter our chief problem. Look
with love as inventory is taken. Weep
for the self-injurious fool for whom blame
was a convenience. We lived for years
in the valley, didn't we? We were right
then! Yes, we were. But how does
being right help us? The internet cannot
change where the trouble starts.
The internet loves blame. Do not trust
anyone who loves blame. For if suffering
is the bearing or undergoing of pain,
distress, or tribulation, then why
increase suffering in the world? Take
that item off the shelf and never
let it down, give it to no one else,
do all good things working against
that weight. Perhaps, carrying the item,
your face will never betray true emotion again.

🖤. Tonglen

I inhale your furies & exhale peace
I inhale wound & exhale peace
I inhale your blame & exhale space & peace
I inhale the child-killers & exhale the children, in peace
I inhale defense & exhale starfish arms spread in peace
I inhale delusion & exhale clarity & peace
I inhale pedagogy & exhale poetry & peace
I inhale ideologies & exhale peace
I inhale convenience & exhale cracked planters & peace
I inhale sadness & exhale sadness & peace
I inhale right & exhale wrong & peace
I inhale wrong & exhale right & peace
I inhale suffering & exhale a little less & peace

🦋 What do we know of the subtler orders?

We know the subtler orders stay quiet for a reason.
Survival isn't a season, but rather our enthusiasm
for remaining alive. Some say unseen, we say
invisibilized: pain not metaphor of damage
or weaponry but deep endurance. Want a blade?
We know you prefer them. I have a canopy instead,
green and more green. A glade. Want a hammer?
Let's visit the hacienda at the end of the world,
where the partial play in peace, not pieces,
stammering out sentences like, *In love with love.*
Our subsistence manifestoes concern life skills.
What "we" does this poem intend? My son. Me.
And all the other men of rain who prefer to be

alone.

> The bodies you view are complete,
> recovering as they cover topics like
> How To Be. Oh immanence of altered
> mind, witness the divine need not to
> heal, but to be, but to be, that is to come.
> Tourist who takes the elevator down
> to the empathy core, this is the place
> we are allowed to have. That it's ours
> is always subject to change according
> to your law. The subtler orders replace
> healing with being so that you can't
> quite hear us, or know how much living
> is going on. Beauty is invisible,
> my loves. Be in love like us, and we will
> show you how to be, unseen palaces.

🏵. Of green & more green

Jab not   the heart is tender
I would hurt no one   wonder

what it takes for all body-
minds to not suffer

Survival must mean more
than this failure to thrive

I love my loneliness, it is
my truest friend, I feed it

water & gluten-free bread
& keep it well-read

guarding what sanity
under a canopy

of green & more green
Worlds are always ending & yet

I am the Fool preferring
the company of trees & my kid

divines ley lines, unseen
highways for bird's eyes

✖ Failure to Thrive

Shame of the marginal face,
of the total spell cast by rain,
of idiot song – I arrest at song,
just syllables, all noise
reduced to meter – and boy
consumed by opportunity's
wolves, a clinger to the lexicon,
survivor of the repeated reckoning
with reduced life chances,
unidentified until an adult –
I make such a good meal
for the fantastic wolves, right now
dressed in sheep's clothing,
as prophets of virtue
and merchants of fortune,
in this, I thrive, failing to be a wolf –
which is failure how, exactly?

A terrible thing to taste

Calling all wolves
let us be unashamed of our
idiot song

I am all noise, no meter
repeating
the divine need

to be to be
changed
by witnessing

allowing Beauty
to alter
minds taste terrible

make terrible waste
not, want not
the virtue parade

& its boring spectacle

Us Ashes

From the other side of extinction
there is emotion. I suffer the quelling

when you ask, *What does evolution*
mean when you're a mutation?

Why evolution as frame when
all I've got is a moment, one

eternity in the Blakean grain?
Why genetics, older brother

of eugenics, when difference
is material, yes, but also more

material than mere? Oh, I am in lieu
– a paradox of intense mood

I cannot identify. As we know,
love's a ruined form. So

we are love's evolved creatures?
Non-mathematical proofs

are the kind I entertain. *We say*
seen when we mean known.

I say seen when I know better.
I say love when I know better,

I keep saying it – to be ruined,
wrecked, what other way to be?

I, too, am *half-sick of shadows*
& of suffering but without

that genetic inheritance I wouldn't
know what love looked like,

I wouldn't know love to know it.
In sickness and in being

I have and hold the abstract
emotions that seek confirmation

in the material world (of course
they seek out bodily referents,

we may not be their metaphors
of lack) but if love is not lack

then my metaphors are dead,
and, proof, this body is not dead.

Not yet. Even then, this body
will be ashes. Furious ashes, on the wind.

🏵. Freaks Like Us

The difference is not in the material,
it is in the perception

of the material,
that there is a *difference*

that must be fixed.
You detect

the subtler emotions,
the tightening of the eyes,

the smothered smirk,
the body's clues betray

another jerk. You know,
you've always known,

it's why you prefer
to be alone.

Some can't help what
they've been taught

until they question
every thought

& who has the time to figure
out ways to be kind

to freaks like us

In Sulci

As quetiapine's dose jacked up, my muscles ached
until the dystonic body bent upon itself, knew wood,
concrete, boron.

I became material, a tetanic object, ecstatically inert –
in pain, muscles tautened to pull against their bones
as if tethered on a bow,

but the quiver ensteeled, yanking weaker flesh –
the whine, the bones, they whine – as the computer
monitor, turned on,

whines – not a metabolic problem, says screen,
nor an enzyme screaming beastly exhaustion in lactic acid
waste, but a brain,

always a brain having strung its receptors like tin cans
along cell membranes – clang, clang, clang, the stigmata
of love,

and oh, excruciating, do not warn the lovers, may they lie
so still with one another, the signal arrested between bodies,
in sickness,

health, and I am the difference between that difference –
some talk of body. I feel a body felled, dense, lying
in sulci, as if surface touch

of vinyl against a back were thick, all through – there are drugs
for this, but I felt it for hours each day to understand
what it means to be a metaphor,

the unmovable object in the marital bed, to know a substance
by its hardness, weight, to be that just by being a poor brain
in lack, in lieu,

suddenly petrified, still despised.

🌹. The Dystonic Body

My muscles ache, tautened to pull against
their bones as if tethered on a bow,
the quiver ensteeled by a spinal cord
stuck in perpetual flinching, yanking
the weaker flesh, bones whining,
whining as they grind a droning song,
tinnitus or something like it, higher,
insistent, a keening wire twisting in
high winds The dystonic body bends
upon itself, forced in configurations
alien alphabets spelling out help in
the nerve's forgotten unspoken language
excruciating the signal arrested in my body,
in sickness & in unsickness. I am
the difference. Yes, there are injections
for this if your skin is thick & inelastic,
able to withstand the treatment,
in other words, insensitive. If it doesn't
kill you, if you don't slacken, sicken
& starve, a heavy blue rose on a frail stem

Adapting to blue

Heavy blue rose of the languid non-dream,
the paranoia-dampener that relieves distress
as petals under the tongue, your language
of rigid stem and wave on the wind is less,
lesser, least; that I'm dying is not the blue,
wrong hermeneutic; that I have a need
to take you under my tongue is mere caress
between two grand misunderstanding shades
of blue, one baby and the other cyanotic.
Each petal melts like a sandy snowflake.
No dreams, for the lovers waken. Blue
because sadness is a stain I can't get out,
like blood and thought, like the genetic
wrong turn made long ago when dreams
were possible but the world made its bargain
and I'm the result, peeking from under
a blanket. Child-killing, love extinguishing
blue, delusory blue – death's palimpsest,
extinguishing clues to calm – for the child
that decided, long ago, to adapt, to redefine
normal as normative and this life
as the deepest dive, a full fathom five,
where fathers lie with legacies of life, of coral petal.

Catch-22

I don't believe in proof

🦋 Home is so Sad

An old man asked on the phone, *How does
it feel to finally be diagnosed as autistic?*

Oh, you know, it's the old problem:
immovable object, irresistible force,

metaphors that Can't and Won't,
but their good intentions are enough –

right? Scream *You give me a word
for pain, I'll use it* and he'd lock me

up. Scream anything and locks gild.
Sitting on a bed, the great avenue

of my life, I said into the receiver:

*It's as if all the words I was once
called as a child coalesced into a single
word, that word, the one for pain –*

but, lacking that word, knowing that
screams are only evidence, not expression –

Grief, I said, *I feel grief, because,
in some way, all the words
the tormentors said were true –*

words closer to pain than most metaphor –

🌣. The Man Who Operates on Brains for a Living

Me: "I don't think you are, I mean, I never thought
anything you did as a baby or little kid was strange
or unusual. Everything you did always made sense to me."

Kid: "That's because YOU'RE autistic!"

Situations slide into place with humiliating force:
the friends I thought, weren't, the names they called me
weren't affectionate, were they? & boys & men,
what they did & said – & the cruelty of the feminine
person is, I mean I get it, but still, astonishing

"You're so literal," as though there's something wrong
                              with expecting accuracy
"You're so literal," as a way to deny actuality
"You're so literal," means you make us feel stupid,
                    have no sense of humour

                    Because all of this is *so* hilarious

"Is it at all possible," I asked the man who operates
on people's brains for a living, "that if a body is constructed
of, for the sake of this argument, weaker, stranger materials,
would it react differently from a body made of the usual stuff?"

Seconds pass in which his unwillingness to commit to a line
of reasoning posited outside of his frame of experience moves
across his face; it isn't true at all, not being able to read faces,
they are painfully clear & that disdain is what makes me avoid
most gazes.

          "Is it at all possible," I asked the man who operates
on people's brains for a living, "that a body made of different
materials can't be measured with the usual standards?"

Seconds pass in which I shift & shift position again, my feet
purpling in mottled numbness, I won't be able to walk,
will have to half-crawl out of here

                              If it's a known thing
that neuroatypical people can't handle fluorescent lighting
why the fuck is every hospital supermarket shopping mall…
I mean why don't we give a shit, why is the world
designed for insensitives?

Gaze Aversion

The truth is, I prefer not to look.

In a person's face are emotions I misplace anyway,
motivations a mystery perfected in poetry.

What do poems mean? Who, what, when, where, why –
the face as detective story.

My world is nonlinear.

In the corner, shadowangles.

The eyes in another's face repel my like pole.

Letters on the table.

Speech reconstituted as sonic properties that become meaning,
echoes in the history of the language.

Yet some unmistakeable energy in being across
from someone else.

I don't look into their eyes, but then eyes lie.

We agree?

How someone feels, though, that fact pushing my eyes
to the corner.

🍂 Like an Animal Stretching in Sunlight

I still can't sit still, am unable
but it's workable, our obstacles
are our oracles, still, I struggle
to settle, shiver under the maple's
branches half-full of brittle fall
leaves that still cling, paper icicles
patched with spring's small
mysteries, sleek black squirrels
eating peanuts like Seroquel,
narrow airways shunt inhales
away from the chest's crucial
hollow, the heart starves to unfurl,
branch out, expansive, like an animal
stretching in sunlight, fearless & natural.

The Terrible Word

Restless, irritable, discontented,
versed in plots the doctor can't know,
I've tried to write the terrible word   (love)
in ways other than any I've known –

        Beauty seems the lie
I've always wanted to believe in,
but can't, quite, as if the desire
to be loved sponsors the poem
I'd most needed, once upon a time,
to soothe my soul. Yet the lie
was disproved too late –

part of the plot to remind us
we could give this thing to others,
steep them, too, in the wonder of holding,
of witnessing them, as the beautiful
things have held me as I dreamed
them according to need.

But: restless, irritable, discontented,
convinced I'm chased, watched,
persecuted – things I must never,
ever admit to medical regulators –
I write myself to the ends of the earth
where love's the miscast quarry
that's out to get me. Yes, it's beautiful –

suffering is the subject of the old masters –

of course – so beautiful that the dark plot
unfurling in front of my face – wife, children,
friends – seemed wounded when I thought
they were, are, out to get me; and –
of course! – this makes no sense,
but that must be added to the list,
the human list, it makes no sense.

❦ If I Were Water, If I Were Fire

I am afraid of water, I am afraid of fire,
I am afraid of drowning & dousing

& have been burnt on the altars of spectacle.
All things fall apart, even the beautiful,

still I wait for the natural, not to touch
or be touched, groundless promises.

My container leaks, I spill & spread,
pretend courage but feel dread,

an inferno consuming my name,
body and history. I know my shame

is common but strain against the knowing,
I love my beautiful child but he has known

so much love we aren't the same species.
I love my beautiful partner but our bodies

don't speak the same language, I'm not sure
we're from the same planet, this one overtaken

by unclimbable high-rises we claim are beautiful
but the truth is *look. Look!* Look

at the misery in the alleys & the ghost forests
& the rivers haunting swimming pools.

If I were water, I would rise & drown it all,
the garish garbage, the shitty shopping malls.

If I was fire I would raze the schools,
jails, hospitals, all the ways we shape ourselves

into tools, into knives. Would that be a kindness?
Senseless not to love the world's neuroses

as my own. I am no different, the horror,
no better, *different, same, different,*

we are all soft bodies bound by breath,
we are all beautiful altars.

❧ The World Assigns an Economic Value for Every Object

Once upon a time, I decided
the world was right.

Though it offered many gifts, I refused them – because
the world was right.

Was this a decision? If
the world was right

(you are worthless, die, just die, everyone will be relieved,
you are not worth the breath you take)

then I had no choice. Do you see? Such was the confusion when
the world was right.

Comfort and distress, love and anger –
the world was right,

I should agree to disappear, bother no one; to be still in the darkness. Yes,
the world was right,

I should expect no succor; I should succumb. And
the world was right,

the poems I write are a dream no one will read.
The world was right,

reading them aloud, laughing, saying: these are the words of a child!
The world was right,

I can expect no better,
the world was right.

If comfort was offered then
the world was right,

I rejected it like a wretch. So
the world was right;

but the world didn't predict you –

🐾 You Save the Ones That Blame You

We need music, we are black holes
of need. Needing to not bother anyone,

hiding by instinct. I am the wrong song
sung by the wrong throat, *I want to go home.*

Some animals are miracles, loving
morning as though born to this planet,

some animals are mothers losing
the instinct to mourn, *This is not*

what I wanted for you, son,
this punishment. I go mad

with wonder, decide morning
after morning to perform the trick

of being without medicine or definition
your mother, your home. Before I go,

please can I go, I will risk, *please let me risk*,
being honest. You must make music

of strangeness, sing the loss
or die hiding. You taught me this

in our little time together, no word
is intrinsically *bad,* no one, even you,

is *bad, so bad, bad.* If I die to keep you safe,
is that mothering, martyrdom, or murder?

Intrinsically bad

I've never doubted a feeling,
having learned they're free

and usually true –
and though many have claimed freedom –

an only life can take so long to climb clear of its wrong beginnings,
and may never,

I wish I could be as sure otherwise
as this one thing,

of worthlessness,

surer even than the love I have for my children.

The world says this, over and over again;
and may never, and may never, and may never, and may never

and the truth of inconsolability is, at this great remove,
that it takes self-pity to be unmoveable

in the face of your words.

Is the paradox this: self-pity as the ravenous consolation?

🐞 This One Unbearable Life

I was trained to doubt all feelings
having learned they're unverifiable

and therefore lies. A lifetime,
that's what we get,

this one unbearable life & yet
it is borne. The world says

I am worthless, *bad, so bad,*
the world wears its hard

heart on its sleeve. I am worn
apart from its belief, I am a worm,

weak & sensitive, am moved
by the least, a mother racoon

removing her babies one at a time
from our neighbour's attic, climbing

down the drainpipe face-first,
an infant dangling from her jaws,

a blue jay's fake crow caw to steal
peanuts from squirrels, how it feels

to learn *I may never, may never,*
may never & my son *may never,*

may never ever. The main effort
is remembering songbirds

in every season, the paradox
of being wretched & beloved.

❧ I believe in the good things

and may never,
and may never,
and may never,

A friend once told me my poems are like prayers

and may never,
and may never,
and may never,

I cry at the broken places, poems cry at the broken places

and may never,
and may never,
and may never,

Let that be written on my gravestone:

and may never.

Its breath hot in our small faces

Everything I say struggles against the vacuum —
others stealing air as if the air sucked
out of the room were from consolation itself,
wresting my testimony *that does not save me*,
that keeps me warm and injured, yet alive,
a monster too strange to behave like one?

Roiling through my face as I write these words
is a whole history of pain prepared, designed,
readied for the breath on a small face now an altar
a priest breathes clean before he transubstantiates
bodymind — which I do love, I do — into a god game.
I want to be consoled but it doesn't make any sense

to me on this earth. The only consolation:
my small face pressed against the asphalt.

❦ White Picket Fences Rickety in Snow

Mouth full of dish towel howling
curled against the cellar door,
be QUIET or get something else
to cry about. White picket fences
rickety in snow, torn screen doors
no defense from the punishment
for being slow, the beatings
my brother got for spilled milk
& how we were taught our pain
was a lie, that we were greedy
for attention. Now I can't pay
attention to being paid attention to
& deflect from me to you, lest I forget
what happens to selfish children.

How to be human

is to see my son,
terrified.

I am angry
because his slowness
has asked
for patience.

I shout –
and see him startle
just like I did once.

No broken place
is strong enough,

none –

it's being my father, me, and my son –

a *selfsame* trinity to form the holy scream

♥. & ♦ Bonfire Beauteous

The five-year-old in light is utopia –
we all crave nests, love, everyone,

we are all enough & need no correction.
Pockets of darkness shrivel; a child's wisdom

is a bonfire, beauteous. I've long thought
the flaw was mine alone, peeking out

from my want through balled fists,
seeing people holding one another, jealous

of the ask & answers in arms. The five-year-old
under the maple tree, hands too weak to hold

each another, the five-year-old hums
herself to sleep each night, alone.

♥. The Secret Truth

When you say need, I hear, I can hear you.
Yes, I have secrets. I'm talking to you,
I know I am, but what are you?
I will you miss you, I believe you,
ask me anything. Yes, I will take care
of you, if you need me, I will come.
Please help me. I love you,
make it better, please bring me poetry,
I'll try not to hurt you & go on hurting you.
You can count on me. I will let you
go. I believe in you. Now. Take what you
want now. I hide between the lines.
I will wait. I will go with fireflies down
to the sea. Those are the words you
know the heart speaks. I am a rare flower.
The path is the plan. I stay in bed,
I try not to think but you know it never
ends, yes, I am high, my problem is pain.
I am sure that I care. You know, I wish
I did not care. You ask because you care.
I'm serious. I can't admit my shame.
I am fallen. Yes. Yes, I am insane,
I am the rhyme's unreason, will you
accept me, I am the physical fact
of the chemical treason. I am, I am & you.
You belong here. Now we can end it,
from the sky comes our deliverance,
or so you say the story tell us, yes,
if it's a good story. I wish I knew. Do you?
Because failure is wisdom's teacher.
You live in the shadow of the upraised hand.
We are meant to be together. The difference
splits us, we should not let it. The ground

is common in every year, we can love
in every season, yes. It is the season
of agreement, we love ourselves fearlessly
& we have no reasons left to argue.

❦ I know I am, but what are you?

I know you are, but what am I –

I, disintegrate in the light, for it was meant to find me;
and being found, the pain was distributed.
When I hear you say

love,

the overwhelmed senses
scream –

the five-year-old doesn't know how to contain that word,
he understands *Want* because it is a system.
Love? He's worn that word around his neck
like a noose,

a partisan on a scaffold –

he has been taught the word
like a scholar –

he knows all the guises and raiments

and when you try to console
the pain rises as do the tides.

I see you as the moon
agitating the earth,
my head against the asphalt
as water rises.

No matter what I want
consolation would be nice,
but that word makes me think of love

and then I want to be better.
I want what others have, consolation,
I want what others do, what you do, consolation,
and I know I'm lost.

🐝 & 🕯 The Moon Agitating the Earth

When I hear you say *love,* the overwhelmed senses scream –
(the word safe *& I'm doubled over, keening)*

the five-year-old doesn't know how to contain that word,
Let it spill, it needs no container, is meant to overflow

he understands want because it is a system
Love is not a system of obligation, it is an ocean

Love? He's worn that word around his neck like a noose
That is unknowing, a love tied tight with abuse

stringing up partisans on a scaffold – *sing torture,*
it unfolds he has been taught the word like a scholar

but a poet needs no teaching, is born knowing
a poet know the guises & raiments of the ideal,

a poet is love's thrall & when you try to console
the pain rises as do the tides *falling, rising, falling, rising*

I see you as the moon *uninhabitable, out of touch* agitating
the earth, *it needs some shaking up* my head against

the asphalt as the water rises, no matter what I want
the water falls, rises, falls, rises, consolation would be nice,

but that word makes me think of love *& its disguises:*
parent, teacher, doctor, social worker, concern.

I mean something better, and then I want to be better,
& desperately want to be better, to eat, walk, laugh, not to suffer.

But human is to suffer. I want what others have, consolation,
I want what others have, consolation & have been offered none

but keep seeking, I want what others do,
what you do, connecting with others, caring.

But I am only a distant satellite
far from home & I know I'm lost.

♟. Intake Questionaire

Where are you going? Can I come too?
What did I do? Why doesn't the pain ever stop?
Why does my body hate my mind?
Will I ever know why?
Why does everyone else know what to do?
Why does everyone else know why?
What does it mean to be loved?
Why is this happening to me?
Why do they keep on hurting me?
Why do they love the engines more
than their children? Why am I so broken?
How much more must I break? Will I bear it?
How much more can I take? Will it keep hurting?
How do I get out of this? Can I get out of this?
Why don't I get to belong? Why is it
so cold? What should I do?
What can I do? What am I able to do?
Is it true? When will I learn?
How can I tell? Will it ever end?
How should I be? How long before they come for me?

Draft answers from the intake board

There is an answer to your questions that begins,
No –

but there is a question you have that we dislike:

Will I ever know why?

We offer *No* like a password to all existence,

we rest our heads on *No* like an asphalt pillow

and sing songs of desolation to the children

to indoctrinate them in loss –

and we really don't know why,

no being the most economical answer anyone can offer –

what people scream when the light comes to destroy them –

the loudest, most piercing sound –

is this your answer?

🐝 & 🕯 The Intake Board Approves Your Application

There is an answer to your questions that begins
No – but there are questions unending,

as diffuse, as infinite, as radiant as light.
There are questions you have that we dislike:

am I all there is, is this it, is it my error,
the origin of all my suffering,

is it like this for everyone, is my pain
singular, am I alone, am I ugly,

will I get it, in the end, will I finally
understand? *Will I ever know why?*

We offer *No* like a password to all existence,
pass exits as we sink in, insistent on existing,

we rest our heads on *No* like an asphalt pillow
slap our pills on the flat salt plains, sow our ills

& sing songs of desolation to the children
as they sing songs of desecration to us

to indoctrinate us in loss –
illness, sadness, softness, hardness,

& we really don't know why,
& are mad with unknowing,

no being the most economical answer anyone can offer –
but what has the economy done for us lately? *Mother –*

what people scream when the light comes to destroy them –
the loudest, most piercing sound ringing in my head,

is this your answer? I have no answers
but unending questions about flowers.

🌹 The Rational Truth

Why does it hurt when emotion spills out of a body?
To remind us that we are alive.

How does emotion spell 'body'?
In extracellular alphabets, in the diamond pulse

      of stars, with a tongue
      we don't speak or even perceive.

What does it mean to be good?
To do no harm upon Earth, to love even the birds of prey.

Why is the surplus of beauty everywhere?
For you were born & we became beautiful in your making.

What is the password?
I am, I am, I am.

Is there always another way?
There is only through & there is only this. & this. & this.

What is the real word for 'real'?
Pinnochio took it to his grave in the grove.

Is there room for one more?
For a billion more, you are wanted, needed & seen.

Is it meant to be?
It could not be otherwise.

What is the subject to time?
Illusions love mirrors, mirrors love alphabets

      & we are all chained to a narrative
      told before we were born.

Why are the painful questions four words long or less?
Love fits the lips.

Why steel, steel, steel?
Because we did not give, give, give.

Where is the path?
It is the long night & longer days full of questions

> & in your breath
> & veins & ribs, in the shadows beneath your eyes,
>
> in the ground down sockets & holes
> where teeth used to be, in the scar tissue & sag,
>
> the path is the pilldust & backless gown
> & the sidewalk littered with cigarette butts,
>
> it's this line & this & beneath your feet & wheels
> & crutches & stumps, it's in the blood you dance in
>
> & your stale breath, cheap cheese dust
> from the vending machine sticking to your hands,
>
> the path is the line & the poem & the word
> & the spit & the shit & you are exactly where you need to be
>
> & always have been, love,
> you have always been going the right way,
>
> the only way is this here & you are home, love,
> you are home.

What is a story?
A trick to make the emptiness palatable.

How much more loss?
As much as the ocean can be drained of, until you are purified

    of your name, your refusal, until you quit
    this stubborn insistence on self as singular,

    until you give in & are undone in the giving,
    until there is so little of you left you surrender,

    until you are broken
    & from the breaking born.

Is this the end?
Love is endless.

Who are the dead?
We are among you, from you, we are your breath

    & you are our ghosts, the wind
    of a thousand haunts & a billion histories,

    a symphony of summer sleeping,
    a melancholic answer to what, October,

    countries chilled by fireflies,
    little light a colony of campers, too distant auroras

    & what blackness we believed
    was endless & not the infinity of colour,

    a coalescing of collected energies, unsorted,
    reborn as what could be a kindness,

    left alone to unfurl crooked or straight,
    curled or lean-lined pretending at linearity.

A this follows this follows this is not.
All at once blades of glass lean pressed together

leaves of moments, windows of years
all occurring, see rising & star fallen,

winter keeps cycling but at once when we know
the winding will conclude, chrysalis & empty,

fullborn & sweetdead, a keep of no need
for answers we kept howing the wise.

Is there a reason?
Yes, no, maybe, as many as stars shining senseless in the sky.

Is it safe?
Never & always. Let go & see.

What remains?
Echoes, fossils, dragonflies in amber.

How come?
Because we refuse to learn another way to be.

What about me?
You are the light without which the universe would cease to exist.

Am I good?
As good as a forest, as good as a river,

as good as a mountain,
as good as a mother.

Where can I hide?
Between the lines.

Am I allowed?
None may permit.

Am I all in one piece?
From perfect wholeness comes perfect wholeness.

Am I alive?
This is your body ribboned from dancing in your own blood.

What's in it for me?
Erasure of self into the starless soulful sea.

Where can I trade less for more?
In kindergarten you trade carrots for candy.

Am I being objective here?
You are the subject of the objective not to be othered, unloved.

Do I have to accept this?
If you want to the pain to cease.

What does my father's face mean?
A child's terror unseen.

Can I escape?
You are the door in & through.

Can I take it with me when I go?
There is no other outcome.

Can I wake up now?
Not without letting go.

Can I see change when it is coming, or only when nothing is the same?
You woke in a snowfield without a name.

What is my role in this disaster?
We are all complicit & innocent.

Did I do the right thing?
Always with love.

Did I mean to?
We are all innocent & complicit.

Am I right or wrong?
You are larger than the littleness of a pendulum.

Did I choose that?
To be wise you chose the lessons hardest to learn.

Am I responsible?
We are each architect of only our own sorrowful cathedrals.

What do I know? All my life: what do I know?
That lessons never end.

BOOK 2:
Empire of Unkindness

🍂 Domestic Terrorism

Grackles fight starlings for the suet in the cage,
"10 calories a day keeps a bird alive," my kid says

after their regular morning stagger & puke,
keyboard clattering. What would Hunter S. Thompson

do is not sage parental anything. The old dreams:
the door breaking between him & me

(my brother's body swinging from a tree)
estimate the damage of persistent memories:

running down the street, my kid heaving in my arms,
no money for a cab, no screen for ambulances or alarms,

checking, re-checking the rise & fall of their chest.
After twenty-three years of fearing death, shelter is another

word for terror, every five minutes a sob sucked in.
We are always dying, have always been, you can feel it,

there's no difference between Dickinson & Whitman
when you get down to the electrons – what is the work

trying to do but be a half-inflated lung, a placemat
for small cats nuzzling your knuckles,

they do what they like, like neurons & smart bombs
& fathers & time. If a screen screams unchecked,

will the AI feel it, the tyranny of narrative?
We have not made this beautiful Earth.

I love the sky emptied of planes,
made things made quiet, the ocean full of light, birds,

city streets re-peopling with animals, small things
grown brave without the trespass of tyrants

Information Overload

Gaze-averted to control information's spigot,
the noise-cancelling earphones slaying
distraction's dragon, I cede to no touch
except the designated, and in designated
spaces, an impoverished gesturehood that relays
a nominal series of explosions across the skin –

with only one way through the world, routine,
sound a soothing tide, like designated
touch, but no way to limit the flow
and so it can be the spike that sets the scream –
just one voice, please, one source
crammed into one metaphor of divergence

♥. Anytime, an anywhen of half-past madness, half-known –

The window is always half-cracked,
that's how we drain your humours

after the light gets in
If desire is abusive burn me

at the stake, I dream of cake &
sometimes of being had

Corner Brook was always strange
after Toronto, I got to play

at being from a big city
So cool you've ridden a subway!

Glossing over fire alarms & garbage,
working at making up, always up

Toronto is strange now, skyline
a contractor's bottom-line

& didn't there used to be a lake?
I followed litterers down sidewalks

as a little kid scolding them
Toronto the Good, clean proud

I didn't know
it was Tkaronto

At twenty-one I'd gone
through so many roommates already,

none survived me long
(I probably still owe them all money)

the two-bedroom at Donlands
over the bakery, the carriage house

in the Annex, the hallway
at Queen & Logan & the basement

at Steeles, couches & crash pads
cardboard boxes & squats

studios & rooms without locks
& the clock that ran backwards

ripped off the wall
at one of those art school parties

Is it so off the wall to try
to dissolve all boundaries

Dunce

Let words reign again as they once did –
not a poet of cripples, but of *fucked
in the head,* face turned corner-ward,
cone on the crown. What was said
way back when? Nothing new under
the sun. *Retard, dummy, tool, not all there,
slow, useless,* I once was a nonce human
of grunt, a corner hum. Stim is the song
of this dunce. At age forty-four, still I case
each room for its corner. How better to know
a place than where to live within it as exile?
Love to corners, the four points that form
the normal shape, squared sharp, my prison
coordinates – I said *love* and I meant it,
because I'm a dunce with no self-pity.
I licked you. I still do. *You were tasty.*
Still are. My resonating hum sent back
at my hated blunt head, blank square
standing on guard for shame at Pixieland
Day Care Centre near Hubbard Avenue
Elementary – ah, the past as sound. *Dunce!*
Once upon a time truth, as monster's
illumination, rose. Fists curled, heated
towards the sound. Yet what was once
said as epithet – *Dunce!* – now means
a hallowed state, inaccessible to you
and in excess of you; our sense of time
not your time; our coeval relation with
objects not yours. This is yours: *Dunce!*
uttered as nonce name of a New Brunswick
quarantine where love continues to grow
strange because it, too, cannot escape
its four corners. Posture as silly-putty,
as Quasimodean hills like white elephants,

as Lurch with a buffalo hump. I love like
this and I *Dunce!* like I love: with fingers
pressed to lips and then to sky which is
a ceiling capping the north corner of my
bedroom, father's wood table blocking access –
You love like *what?* How am I in love?
Like this: standing on guard in the corner
for beauty itself, as ugly transpires. *Dunce!*
Ugliness of normal life. So many similar
grunts overheard, but coordinated as laughter.
Not understanding corner pedagogy – an
infinitely recreated asylum, compass points
marking normietown – I wanted love but
learned to hate my difference. Let's call
their reason beauty. So I stood in the corner
with shame. *Dunce!* Let us recover then,
you and I, with the ceiling as our sky.
Why ask why of darkness? Do this with me,
now. Identify a corner in your bedroom.
Stand there for half an hour, as close
as you'll get to being a dunce & beauty
for love prefers the conical hat. Slur
manifestoes of being in love with love;
we mutter *In love with love* with lisps,
stutters, muffled; call us simpletons. *Dunces.*
Go ahead. For we're in love, and not like
you at all.

🍄. Raise Giant Mushrooms In Your Cellar!

that snuffed-out light as my pillow,
under the cover of
difference –

"I bet you read the dictionary for fun,
no one likes a snot-nosed stuck-up

know-it-all brat, why'd you get
an A-minus not an A-plus, teacher's pet,

have you read every book in the library yet?"
I hadn't until Ms. Madill left

The Machineries of Joy on my desk,
a Bradbury-ian mushroom given light at last

or at least interstellar flight
to flee beery cheque day fights

& the every-other-nightly breakdowns
& beatings, see me fake sleeping,

growing skinny & strange, ungrounded,
& that word deliverance? Unfounded.

Let's call the whole thing off

Oh yes, deliverance as if the angel
took a tree stump and cracked it
open with his hands, saying,
This I do in memory of all
the broken covenants this world
formed with care. No one watches
the demonstration, no one cares,
not knowing the words for love
or the act itself, preferring
a deliverance from pain
that is common & no deliverance
at all, because that's the problem
with the frame. If you want pain,
then think of cure. But if you want
love, then suffer from want
and be ready for the sundering.

❦. Does Something Wicked This Way Come

You never get used to the sensation
of falling – the Buddhists say it's okay

to not get used to anything.
I cling to delusions of judgment

like I hated rapists & racists
abusers & accountants,

the hornet's nest of politics
I hung on to with bleeding fists,

hating Bad Men & misogynists
but what I hated most

was my own shadow projected
on the world's cave wall.

I used to hate living, witnessing
so much pain,

I used to hate but without the tyranny
of the terrible

the beatboxing monk's heart sutra
wouldn't be viral

Oh Empire

Oh empire, sick provenance,
blood cough, broken teeth,
and the fists dragging across brick –

Oh love I feel the same way,
not knowing a thing except at
the intersection of feeling and sound –

my daughter's voice penetrates the empire,
asks for coordinates,
but I'm hiding –

From the other empire,
I hear her singing a pop song softly,
the song's signified heart an icon that,

I implore,
is no empire unless
I never loved a thing –

I have loved to know
sound arranged like a march,

blood embittering the ground
that cries out resentment as a word,

Why –

the love-hum underneath that nourishes
the grave,

dead loves at attention, their knowledge
reduced to anthem,

the flags at half-mast for the empire of love.
And we choke out the song.

It hurts to breathe through the heme –

they knew it was true, everyone I've been close to,
this love was ferocious and hated to be quiet

to hear the tutelary hum

O Empire

The tutelary hum drowns out the song,
drones on the wrong programs, makes us numb

Blood coughs, broken teeth, fists dragged across brick:
we are sick to accept this   is not love

Flags, mass graves & guns   O empire,
we are sick coordinating hate with costumes,

staging our outrage in popular anthems
I implore us   stop stay soften

but is it suspect to count myself among us,
nothing about us without someone's opinion

upsetting the apple cartwheeled out of the garden
if you prefer that artful version of our origin,

O no I won't claim multiplicity unless I am
the royal we interrupting this scream of frustration,

gnawed-off   embittered   at its crux
the ferocious hum-love & of course

you hated to be quiet, it's unnatural, the child
who finds it fine to sit in lines of silence

is the empire's pride & join me in mourning
knowledge traded for infotainment, coins

with our faces emblazoned on every free surface
like skin & flowers, not the thing

but its outer   upper   answers to questions
that don't need asking

◀ Suspect to Count

1. I'm here.

2. I forget why.

3. I'm glad to forget.

4. There is no accounting for me,

5. or anyone, anything, abuse.

6. Lists, coordinates, & palimpsests

7. mark my sins down. Oh,

8. I won't repent.

9. They have nine stones to throw, nine.

10. Sound the tin bell.

11. The hell I have within is a disabled alarm.

12. My crazy cousins, aught autistics,

13. marshall screams for ice cream that runneth down our chins.

14. They said nonsense before we did.

15. I make sense but have never been known.

16. You know where pain grows.

17. And all the fancy multisyllables

18. make the age of majority.

19. I was in love! It doesn't count?

20. No, dealer wins.

21. Love is not the only thing, fool,
    stop counting.

🌂. It Takes a Community to Abuse a Child

One, two
Unbuckle pants

Three, four
Lock the door

Five, six
You know what comes next

Seven, eight
Try to run away

Nine, ten
Home again

Eleven, twelve
Dig & delve

Thirteen, fourteen
To court again

Fifteen, sixteen
Where have you been?

Seventeen, eighteen
What will the neighbours think?

Nineteen, twenty
Empty belly busy streets

Disabled Love

In love and in love, I said to COVID,
I said *In love in love in love* –

like my son says, *In love and in love*
with love I'm in love with love

and I don't follow the poets anymore,
they are not *in love with love and love*

is in love with love it prefers its kind
its own self its reproduction its cleaving

and cocooning and spooning, spoons
and cocoons and clefts and my son,

he's spelling m-o-o-n moon
on the sidewalk, and h-a-p-p-y happy

and I ask him to *spell love* and he says *no*
you just want me to and I say *it's love*

I want for you and he says *okay*
and I give him the capital letters,

L-O-V-E,

it's as if I said (p-a-i-n) but he doesn't know
that, he just lives it like me, we too

in love with love and it's love that
we're in love with, love, the poets

won't say love but I will say love,
L-O-V-E, on a suburban street,

to Toronto I shout love as fully wild
and domesticated strange,

as loving being, as L-O-V-E T-H-I-N-G,
and he's humming it now too, bent with chalk,

making a big green blotchy heart, *in love*
with love I'm in love with love in love

with love and love in love with
love and love its love and love is love.

🎯 Unseen Birds

Let there be beds, blankets, needful things
not the tyranny of technology & screens,

protest performed by companies,
words mixed in clearer air, dissolved

in the current where we are all survivors
of the song, this is not forever

or even long, but a pause
in possibility. Perfect beauty is painful,

pain is beauty's perfection, no one
owns a river, remember & change the past

with each glimpse back, a companion
fashioned by iteration into black

breathless stillness. Through the window
a starred sky is soldered over birds singing

unseen in the night's dark garden

Into Black

The prophecy –

You wanted to be good, and are,
but the words used to describe me

were the words from Empire –

love by all the wrong names,
I knew you *this* way

at the cross – what wasn't true in language
and yet the words, as lies, were recognized –

less kindness or the imperative for same,
less care or quiet,

not even space surrounding the selfsame
empire

but this instinct:
no one wishes you alive,
you are worthless,
get out of my sight.

I learned to hide from the empire of sight
and having grown strange in the darkness

I learned the words to the song perfectly,
more practiced:

die, die, die.

The overwhelmed ground
digs its own graves

and hums during excavations

🕯. To Unbecome

What survived
& is good
is poetry

the rest
prophecy
to unbecome

lazy useless
selfish stupid
& other words

I thought
were
love

🦋 And how strange

that the other words for pain were
equally convincing in their turn
– not lies, exactly, merely collateral
damage, the destruction of bodies.

If the other words for pain didn't say
what they meant or speak plain,
then:

      envision the Great Kindness
when love is finally recognized as care,
only care, the synonyms known as lies
buried in an old country we, now
emancipated, can't recognize
for its scars

      – and the scars,
      they *are* love, beautiful –

         o beautiful, lovely, tell me that you reject
         the love-lies now, so clearly false –
         lazy, stupid, useless, selfish, stupid?
         We learn as we go. This is not love.

But, pray tell the painful that their episteme
was designed to betray their bodies?
That the words are tragic failures
of proximity, the near-miss of a glass
of water in the desert? Live by the sword
and the body dies by that language-brandish.

No, the tragedy of the synonyms for pain
is that they come close enough, their imperfection
a greater betrayal.

Lazy, stupid, useless, selfish, stupid? Not love,
but pain mimics, yes?

Body as metaphor,
weapon as metaphor,
damage as metaphor?
What are friends for?
The future, as enemies?

Body in pain,
body of pain,
body with pain –

oh sad fragile body, we must compare
you in the absence of perfection.
I usher in magnitudes of distraction:

*stabbing burning crushing branding ripping
sharp dull ache,* oh, irresistible force
unmovable object unbridgeable gap

& who can enumerate all the metaphors of damage,
the infinite ways a body can be expressed
as injury?

These words signify sensations felt so acutely,
who can say, truly, that they are lies?

The problem of pain is not that we have it,
the problem is we have few metaphors
that are true. The problem is that we'll sing
of lack of language rather than renovate.

Beauty in excess, the scarred plains,
so much beauty, poets,
the millennia rioting,
and who among you has the truth?

🌹. Light Leaks In

There is no test devised that everybody
passes, the devil's plaything is device.

Metaphor
obscures.

Literally thin-skinned, in another world
they would have said I had the Sight

instead of tranquilizing
unblind eyes.

I cannot grow a thicker hide
to save my life. Light leaks in

and I have no choice but to "see"
& yet – privileged to be disabled,

I would not have
such luxury,

would have died on the streets
or worse, I mean,

we do that at home
but now I get running water

& am mostly left alone.

The Sight

The child reached out and said, "No."
At the end of the earth – point B –
when difference meant merely being
understood as same-but-different,
that the epithets intended to segregate
the bad minds from other minds
were just other words for pain
we enjoy and bless for reasons
we metaphorize, that Freud calls
the death-drive and a metaphor
called the devil calls fun, but out
of not understanding, I just run –
until, one night, I rend out the sight
known as fight-or-flight, the extra-
sensory perception that saves
my fucking skin from the trouble
ritually shoved at difference, to trip,
to sink, to trap, to hurt – but at the end
of the earth, the child has nowhere
else to run, and no inclination.
The soundless dark of Exhibition Park
taught me the circle has infinite start
and return points, a palimpsest
of point A to B. Can you see me
with your apprehension, a kid hiding
behind a tree, or in leaf piles,
doomed to be scared and sad until,
at the apotheosis of B, an assumption
of B, the child reaches out
to the assailant and says, *You hate*
yourself, I see, I know. No. That no one
sees doesn't matter. Point B believes.

❧. The I That Eyes Outside

I'm not the I
I was.

I die
a little more
each time –

here, inside
I hide the I
that eyes

the trees
& flailing

grinds
itself against
description,

There is no
I to fix
or find.

No I or Fix

I feel
I feel no
I feel no shame.

I say
I say this
I say this in an upper room with no audience.

All the lies, they can be rejected,
but being part of pain
they make the body cry out for being so desecrated.

I feel
I feel no
I feel no shame
but I feel the other register – for pain is generative.

Of one breath and then another,
of co-creation, of assumed
presence – of song,
all song. After a reading,
a poet asked me, *How
would you define your poetry?*

and rather than deconstruct the question,
posture with other language games,
feign an interest in their self-definition,
or quote anyone else,

I said
I said this
I said this as if I were in the same upper room with no audience,
the daily room:

The poetry I write is a song I carry into battle,
stronger for the wounds as the wounds are wrung
out in the sun, as song —

I
I yet
I yet endure

not weapons or war or damage
but having to be, accepting that,
and refusing to agree to die.

Look, fix
Look, no I
Look at cause:

the little boy, blanket to his head,
sings himself to sleep
under his breath,

a rise and fall that can't be detected.
You think he's dead,
but he's singing unheard.

Breathing, but you see no proof;
singing, but you hear none,
thereby discoursing on pain as expert, master, & revelation,
as counter to the tutelary hum.

♥ No One Is An Expert In Anything Except Their Own Pain

stronger for the wounds as the wounds are wrung
out in the sun, as song —

I feel shame in every organ
left in my body & mourn

their theft
Pain is being part of

the body as it is desecrated
with less care

than we show a text
Deconstruct

everything
define nothing

especially not
poetry

But even that is too definite
here just this

no-birth &
no-death

I know no other way to be, this kind of mourning

So beautiful, your own version of the non-song,
and yes, one learns to mourn the desecrated
body and somehow cherish its incomplete
desecration. But my lowly station as *this*
kind of poet – instilled in me as a charge,
from long ago, a trauma current that flows,
those that have met me know – is to rise and try
to draw blood again for the good, I blurt out
my common truths and crash into the obstacles
as if monsters were invisible, that no one
can spot difference despite my long experience
of being spotted, with actual spots. Comic admission:
I believe that being fearsome delays desecration
a little longer, at the risk of performing it myself.
But this is the relation between body, desecration,
and world: the cost is we either fight, don't,
or decide that there is another way, neither
better than the other, neither better. If I retire
let Caesar at the last render his thumb at half-mast
as I try to vault the ledge and make my way
to his throat, singing the nonsense song designed
for a boy on my lap. Fight or flight my lord,
you are the only emperor of this empire in sight.

🐝 Nothing & Less

It is all contingent, co-arising,
the conditions of our living,
we are all different in
the dark red dark, hanging
on the rise & the fall
of a small blanket
on a small chest at 3 am,
administering medicines
in drudging ignorant
love, I know nothing
& less as I grow toward death
& that unknowing spreads,
if I could rest, gentle
my limbs & limbic system,
could I be beautiful too
now that we're all dependent?

🦋 Could I be beautiful too?

I hear this question on the baby monitor,
the small and tiny voice as breath
overlay on the window showing,
in its turn,
darkness —

the world has taught me,
die die die,

the world has taught me,
the world has taught me

that in love, I am as close
to death as I can be,

expectant,

and in my daughter I see
too much beauty for the song to be true,

a disproof —

no the world says to me as familiar, *die,*
but she is not of that saying,

and I am convinced:

yes, I'm caught in a dissociation,
this relation when I loved as much as death will claim us,
the zenith —

Long ago, something went wrong
and time can't catch up to stillness,

the empire of crack stretching from the broken hand
to the smashed dream,

– and I am responsible for both! –

kernel of here,
the pause before exhalation

🏵. Could I be beautiful too?

The world has taught us
we have no choice,
the world has taught us,

say it with me,
I have no choice,
they taught me

when I was small
& later in my 20s 30s 40s
die die die.

No choice in the first place

The mystery: that a poem is undirected,
aimed one way or another for all the wrong
reasons, uselessly, or all the right ones,
the poem doesn't care. For beauty and truth
have no purpose except to venerate mystery.

Look at the beautiful thing! Admit you can't
know it, you can only damage or care for it.
But know it? We don't have a choice about
this. The mystery is: poems have the *Wisdom*
to educate us, but we need to not listen first
in order to learn.

Realizing we're not here to learn, or to know,
except to make choices for ourselves, we yet aim
ourselves like poems for all the wrong reasons,
uselessly, and all the right ones. The mystery arrives
as a visitation: we stare, quietly, and know less.

Are stilled. We wanted what our choices led to.
By some odd miracle, we learned what poems
led us to with their breadcrumbs: accommodation,
accepting the choice – and only then was it choice!
in the first place –

❧. My anvils my hammers, their mitochondria

Everybody dies –
you, me, sons, flowers, this pain

everything will die.
We get a lifetime

a thousand years, a second,
how are we living in this moment

in this breath
& are we really *here*

with every fiber of our being
when another being needs us

or are we shutting down & spinning out?
That's okay. everybody does it

& we can unlearn it, exchange self
for other: my anvils, my hammers,

their mitochondria.
I love my negativity & equally

my positivity but find the either/or
top-heavy,

the neural habits like a life
sentence set in my spine.

Maybe it's miracles
we need to redefine.

Redefinition of the miracle

Where all is lost and reconstituted,

not the miracle,
not the miracle,
not the miracle

but the simple fact,
how could it be,

and why – not love
or care or what passes
for human,

but when the child knows
they can choose the dust
and make angels,
devils,
castles,
& other names for love

🌸. God of Memories & Flowers

Once upon a time
we were guardians of the grove
in love with love

the ideal of, freedom,
the god of memories & flowers,
shelter for the tired traveler

from songbees in the ruined towers,
succor for the weary healer
refusing Death in Her splendour,

repose for the silence language
has stolen, now nervous
in the presence of self,

reflected-self,
flagellation as promotion,
fixated, jaded.

🕯 Sacred Technician

The little body, washed;
cleaned; swaddled;
transferred
from broken hand
to broken hand
to crib –

I write in sadness as authentication,
but this act is not sacred.

What is sacred: the little body
of finite breath

independent from me,
frantic on its own rhythm.

I listen as
technique

to confirm the child is not dead,
not dead now,
not now,
no –

the moment I share
as witness
an infinity of withheld wait,

an oscillation,

oh little body,
you curate the air
and I worship your sound.

What is the difference between a nose pressed against the glass
and my broken hand passing you to another broken hand,

the transfer,
you little technician

converting my hands into what my father's were –
rotting cathedrals in the rain,
you the stained glass

🎗. Sacred Authentication

Care is sacred,
a cathedral moment
transferring

from unbroken hand
to unbroken hand.
We are all whole

holy is every little
interdependent body.
Do you answer the call

when the other
cracks open
or is that unprofessional?

Listen
not as technique
but in authentication,

   human
to human
unfurl

To imagine exclusion

I felt the human passed to another human,
broken hand to hand (the sacred technique
called reckoning), the calloused chokehold,

the torch, be yours to hold it high,
of my neck —

we cannot exclude what we have already excluded,
the arrangement of social space by opportunity
hoarders — and we call this failure of imagination,
or universal design?

There are two kinds of readers,
those that exclude pain and those that read pain in
because they are nodes too —

why read and exclude oneself,
perhaps it is easier to do so, for awhile

imagine a world that cares for itself,
at the top of an office building,
the owner of the world lets down her hair and says,
Climb up, oppressed!

It's a wig, slip

Mock pain is real pain and anger
is the voice of real pain until

I imagine what it would be like to have none,
and then the feeling becomes a sound

through a monitor,

                                        breath.

All imagining becomes listening,
thus it is written,

by hands that yet reach for necks.

🏆 We're All Losers

There are two kinds of readers in this world:
the kind who believe there are two kinds
of readers & the rest

practice resting
in between the neither/nor.
I felt the human passed to another human,

passed to another human passed to another
human passed to another human

past & future illusions,
no one owns the world, Chuck
we're all losers because

there is no game.
Systems are the failure
of our imagination, no one needs

delusions of property
or economies or isms.
Nodes of pain necrotize,

unlanced, infect
the body politic
to land with boots on necks,

listen, listening is the task
of sacred technicians.
Turn off the monitors

& take
the little bodies
in your arms.

🐦 Empire of Unkindness

Silence is complicity
poetry tells me, loudly,
repeatedly

in the same words heard
during the Great Leap Forward.
Aren't we bored of being boring,

grimly repeating & repeating
guns & germs & steel & wheels
within wheels within wheels?

Each spring a cycle of violence
& pride, uprisings of wrong &
wrong & righteousness swiftly

switching sides, shards
of toppled statues substrate
for just another empire

of unkindness. How many people
have to die before we realize
that no amount of money

is worth a single human life.

In my righteousness

I'm well within my righteousness
to tell you
off,

I'm well within my righteousness!

At some point, all listening
is nose against the glass,
a disembodied desire –

Sure, I'll tell you what to do!
I demand action –

When the revolution comes,
and I am installed president-of-no-one-but-this-office-must-be-filled,
everyone will have a football they can rescind at the last minute,
because they are well within their rights.

Love, we take you back,
your non-empire,
and we recreate you in our own image,
which is fire.
I command the fire not to burn me,
but at the last minute –

🌹 In my righteousness

I preach mindfulness
& peace, Pema says

the protestor sliding the flower
down the barrel of the gun

is the aggressor
& no one wonders:

how scared was the kid
with his finger on the trigger?

I reach agreements with myself
to keep following the path,

keep hacking through the undergrowth
of hopes dashed & broken

glass. Revolutions
are so boring, no one

needs another roundabout
to burn down – how about

we try growing
each one of us opening

& owning our own pain
& holding space

The Pride Cycle

If anyone tells you how to be good, run.
Take this on good advice. Iron encases
the fires that make irony burn. Love,
Ecclesiastes's sun says there's nothing
new under the successor. Sure, desire
has made me a holy fool – we're cheaters,
liars, & murderers with religious cures
to mask the obvious fact of our original
baseness. We wear masks now to protect
other people's faces from uncovering
our unholy bases. Do I sayeth I am in love?
Forsooth: I do. But not like you: my morals
are back in the subsistence cave where I
bunk with my son. The new life forgets
care and sings shame at the top of lungs.
Kaz and I, we breathe so quietly,
you can't hear us sing. I write poems
as offering. He eats peanut butter
on hamburger buns, a dollop of honey
to finish. What the fuck are you doing
with your lives? Have you not enough
overcoming to do yourselves ? We're so
dirty, he and I, for lack of running water.
But before I fully claim the holier-than-thou
terrain of the hatred masquerade, let me say:
in all its guises, pain grows strangest
in the shade. This I know, I agree.
Come visit us and you will see. Call us
prisoners in lieu, of lack. Take pictures.
I'll know you by the flash. You better
run when I see you. You better run.

🏵. The Humble Cycle

If anyone tells you
how to be good,
remember
they're repeating
a cycle
& believe
they're doing good
by repeating
the cycle
of feeling
not good enough
& projecting
outward
what they were taught
by the people
who were taught
how to be good
by the people
who felt they weren't
good enough.

♞ Black Sky

Outside the rain is falling on the canopy tent
I got for Father's Day – forecast called
for tornadoes but I said, *No, let's leave it up,*
I want to hear the sound of heavy rain
on the plastic –

                I'm watching to make sure
the structure doesn't blow away – rain
penetrates the mesh sides; so far the roof
is holding –

black sky is the only safe kind to look at,
for it shrouds the fire with a protective layer,
as if there were a single kind of weather
that was safe for the delicate souls,
the worst kind, when disasters cannot cover
for abuse and we'll survive knowing
the worst is not this, the worst was clear skies
and someone else's cheerful attitude.

🌷. Unmeant Garden

You, too, can be a black-eyed Susan
in a livestreamed zoo, orchids blooming

in curated Zoom windows, set just so
on a bookcase blazoned with titles

we want you to think we've read.
The body hurts even unglimpsed,

dreams of knowing love-making
or of the day I write *love-making*

& mean it, don't wince once, gone
out the window with my shoes & bras

& button-down anything. Privilege is able
to get off using its own two hands.

The Russian sage still dormant in June,
Joey's clones, Chemdawg & AK47

droop in the old pond's shadow,
wormwood wilts, sere anise hyssop pallid,

sad sag gloomy, bedraggled, scarcely
remembered. Dream & the world

is indistinguishable the sages say,
I learned my ugliness early

& cannot sleep deeply enough to dream –
men have kept carving my body

to invent a garden of flowers
where none was meant

◀ The sound of steps

after Alden Nowlan

I don't know if this makes sense,
but being something I've done all my life,
I feel the need to tell you
the secret

that can't be undone,
for it was love that taught me

                                        feeling, sound,

the wrong kind,
but still love –

(we've been over this, I know –

I can't help that my nose is against the glass,
always)

the secret
that though I am the largest in my house,
I walk the softest,
unconsciously,
and I know the gait of my family:

                                 Aria (quiet, irregular)
                                 Kaz (heavy, chaotic)
                                 Zee (light, efficient, quick)
                                 Janet (even)

I can tell who's moving on different floors –
I learned this to survive,

if I have a garden, it isn't silent,
it's not within or of my body,
it isn't trespassed.
For in the imaginary garden, everyone is invited.
Everyone, make the solitary sound
impossible to hear
by your numbers.

🏵️ The Sense of Trespass

My whole body hurts
from a lifetime

of guarding against
tremors

in the floorboards
tip-toeing

on broken feet
& no not everyone's sole

is shattered eggshells
still

we all
know trespass

us, the idea – an inner pariah that, abject,
asks for forgiveness from the entire world
and is denied. So refused, the idea grows
to encompass the grounds of refusal.
Whom cannot be redeemed? The idea
of us is the grounds for pain, and we play
in the playground of us. We sing little songs
because there are at least two pariahs
to sing along. Who could be so shameful
that one is enough? The scapegoating
must be serial, the scapegoating
is Prestige TV. Shame needs a secret
sharer, otherwise there can be no knowledge
of the depths. Oh, we were so very very very
bad, and yet – you did it too! The system
wanted a host of pariahs ostracized
on a reality show island. The system
named all the names, made us known
to one another. The new abuse is the old
kind formerly known as *Goodness*. Yet,
as idea, we can never die. We can never die!
They did not count on that. They account
for all sins, but they did not count on that.

❧. Too Much Begetting

What if there were no sins,
if we were washed clean
of the concept, what could we be
without that stolen mythology?

I haven't read the bible yet,
too much begetting, or the Quran
or other holy books but absorbed
through Sunday school, advertising,

enough shame for all lifetimes.
It took root early & spread like
a demon, set up residence
in my nervous system, mutating,

breeding offshoots each time
a teacher, a doctor, a parent,
an elder, an officer regurgitated
their own poor conditioning,

grafting guilt like fruit to the ganglia.
We do it too, I did it to my kid,
each time I hid or tried to & failed,
the pain, need. Redeem thyself,

be free of needing
redemption
from any being,
& find yourself freed.

Snark Hunt

Yes, the abuse practice, it is everywhere,
in everything, like death – first witnessed
as my father's ability to gift death to those
in his presence – a breathtaking power
no one understands when I explain
but which I feel in my throat, even now,
writing these lines – and that this power
was called love is the fault – with all
the names repurposed to truth, we can
all agree, we can celebrate our newfound
truths and congregate in palaces
of perfect surveillance and shatterability
where our neighbours choke their wives
for not lying – the utopia of care
is my hellscape of ground glass –
please, everyone, join the fight, let's call it
a snark hunt and laugh as we stay on guard
for the possibility of monsters among us,
let's grant original sin its one moral success –
the chance to say

> *Yes, we are all glass*
> *and must handle with care,*
> *let us not forget*
> *the fragile vase*

❧. Dewdrops, snowflakes, stars & spires

The gelid rime of forests frozen
in the peeled-back eye
mine the gardens,

subvert the tired
dewdrops, snowflakes,
stars & spires

before the fisted
sigh leaks out,
torques the spine

into a snail shell
inclined toward the abyss.
Science abuses its license

to deny the subtleties,
simplified: despair demands,
we abide.

⚡ End of the world soliloquy

You seem so wise, so quiet & kind.
Are we at the end of the world,
on the other end of a phone,
listening in the last five minutes?

If so, I am glad that it's you,
I need quiet & kindness to the very end,
it's a good way to die.

Me? I rush from fire to fire.
enforcing its condition.
Next to the fire, I've learned its *Wisdom* – that it is the original

breath,
monitor,
waiting,
action,

but not love,

love is no fire.
I want nothing to do with that.

I am fire
and so know the lie,

rushing from fire to fire and adding to the heat.
Oh please,

fire licking at the breath monitor,
fire also saying *Please*,

wishes made of flames –

the righteous come with torches,

I hear their steps.

I run there, as I've sworn,

deputized to scream, *Selfsame!*

The glass –

🐝 Next to the Fire

Wisdom is easy
on paper –
it's always

the end
of the world
but never

wait here,
next to the fire
on the other end

of the line.

🌶 Contranym

As apologist for an apology
never uttered, I too wonder:

is there any other song I can offer?
I bolt from the bed, bound

to this body except cleaved
by mind. Who wants to hear,

over and over, *This hurts?*
But what of the little girl

who falls, this her
first thought, at great intensity?

The books filled with enumerations
of pain, in this I am like

all the successors. Although –
and I apologize – if nothing

is new, then perhaps nothing
should be new with us.

A therapist said, once,
Just say yes for an entire day,

see what happens. The revolution
based in pain, what pain militates,

became walking to the park,
peer of the noble martyrdom,

what a man might need
to cleave from a body,

or to bolt dust to his bed.

♥. Just Say Yes See What Happens

Yes. Yes to pain I bow

bolted to the bed, bound
by buckled limbs, sound:

mourning doves' fast wings
skinning the rocky ground

dry hiss, leaves, discursive
whispers – I miss less

if I let the weather in
continue to give out useless

everything, who wants to hear,
over & over

this hurts

the unfixable howl.

Less deny than any

In this, I rest as unknowing –
unpliable, without give,
inflexible by medical definition.

I'll say no to the ends of the earth,
to those ends I'll travel
for the chance of denial –

No one wants to hear it, no one loves this imposition –

But no –

You are in love, I think;
in the healthy way

and I am in love with the no of survivorship,
the no of the non-song,
the lover who cannot sing in harmony
with the sky or the lap,
the screech of the needle across those tableaux,
no,
some qualities cannot be extracted,
are infinite –
less refusal than fused,
less deny than any,

it hurts all the time and if there is a limit to listening
then how can there be a limit to pain?

❦ Chrysanthemums

So many words that mean
both peace & desolation
like *please* & *help* & *home*

& *love* in all its reds: blankets,
staircases, bankruptcies, supper
on the table at a certain time

on an unmatched set
of disinherited dishes,
soccer matches, funerals

in other languages,
so many words for death
& isolation, November,

rosehip, chrysanthemum,
mud-luscious streams
of white petals, old songs

on the radio, the hypnotic shush
of windshield wipers whisper
the old dream: *save me, save me, save me please*

🐦 Save Kit

I titled a memoir *Saving*

and that didn't save me,

though I obviously wanted it to.

Detail, detail, detail –

My heart always says,

you need details to save you,

for your philosophy

will not save you.

Or is that my art speaking?

Poetry erupts in flower,

and the charm ensues.

🏵 The other name for I want to die

Crutches are beautiful
if you can clutch them, all

the ways to be unable
are obstacles, consolation

pries up patio stones
to build a shrine for birds.

Safe I don't understand
the word *safe*, fear

of the razor's mess, finger
on the emergency button

eager for an answer or
a cleaner. No one has ever

wondered dared to care
to ask if I was safe –

🌑. Indistinct From Sparrows

White petals
have their own larynx,
ditto purple, black & pink,

every colour has a flavour
& a voice that is distinct,
every tearfall is a tincture

but we're fearful
of the rupture of our "normal"
on the brink, Uncle Nature

wants to touch you,
wants to crush you,
wants to crack you

like a dodo egg, sad dad
indistinct from sparrows
to a little girl, indistinct

from sky, self, flowers
named & not, to a little kid
everything's a teacher, god,

& other names for birds & love

❧ Today I was asked on Zoom about fatherhood

and I can never read a room,
but I spoke of what else –

love –

of my misapprehension of fire,
of scorched earth chasing sparrows into the horizon,
and bedtime stories with three nouns suggested by the child,

of the backyard,

of anaphora as a way to organize the world
as the hospital is organized by bureaucratic list.

I list sideways as a ship
taking on love.

I can never read a room,
but nonsense is the language of children,
and so,
solemnly,
I spoke a nonsense
of futuretrauma
and backwardspeak,
of a breath monitor's passionless hiss
and the caress of rain, rain meant for the wild creatures.

Have you felt the rain beat and then sputter on your skin?
Do you, too, listen to the roof?

Sound and feeling
of the rain,

I have all the names.

🍀 Heart Sutra Remix

Have you felt the rain beat & then
sputter on your skin?
Do you listen

to the roof
noise devoid of origin,
the raw texture of the air

conditioner, humidifier,
refrigerator, wires full
of fear & hate?

This room smells
of old sweat, terror,
roses & Voltaren.

No one calls but sparrows
singing nonsense in the language
of children & flowers –

sound is all sense dissolved
or so I keep hoping.
The hypnotherapist

on the headphones
will whisper psalms,
sutras remixed

by a beatboxing monk,
my neighbour's leaf blower.
Traffic on the commuter

highway is hawk calls
& horns, high-pitched hums
& lawn mowers,

tremor in my bleeding gums
sparks behind my left eye
wild creatures on the horizon.

No,

but how lovely. Those noises
are distraction, a melodious yell
into thought. I need the boring,
regular, paced, and dependable.

When the small terror came
as a child, head under the blanket,
there was one reprieve from outside:
the gently smacked tin, sluicing –

the sound soothed, and I was allotted
only one recoup. Thus, for safety, I soldered
the sister sound from adulthood – the lullabye –
to the rain-sound and decided
if I could not mimic the rain on eaves,
then a nonsense rhyme with words
interchanged, yes, that would do –
a poetry of regular rhythm, I'll tell you
the words soon,
only my son and I know.

You have such beautiful sounds
as atmospherics. Have you adjusted
to the world as it is, accommodated
its sonics, so to speak, a *Wisdom*
in that flexibility? For the world,
it lacks lullabies.

Yes, the lullabyes, they soothe,
but are also early warning systems
of *selfsame* soot silking the horizon –

Yes,

the soothing sound
of a tin roof
is the song

& thoughts
are distraction.
I love the boring, being boring

regularly corrals
the ceaseless terror of being
in an undependable

bodymind, deciding
daily to remember
to love the little

miracles:
a fifty-pound bag of peanuts
bought with Trillium money

will feed a lot of grackles
& squirrels. I adjust
to each shift in the wind

& readjust – if I soften
my hearing: garbage truck,
toddler crying, highway traffic,

fire engine, ambulance siren,
freight train, jackhammer,
airplane, steamroller

all reach & expand
beneath, above,
all birds & nearly silence

🌷. In Which We Fail the Voight-Kampff Test

The hospital is organized
by bureaucratic lists.
I list sideways like a ship

taking on water –
"Why don't you want a wheelchair, honey?"
Orderlies pop up like

whack-a-moles at every exit.
I can't think or speak or see straight
or use my hands or feet –

to wheel a chair or fix my face
to greet the incessantly
well-meaning & their thick-skinned

inability to see more than
sightistly makes me drown,
grind to an end –

"You can't sit here, lady."
No one is responsible,
everybody's hands are tied.

Bureaucracy is a screen
to keep from feeling
other's pain

nothing more than *tears in rain*.

Schematic

Look, the girl drew a picture.
A blue crayon line rises to the top
of the page and off. Another
meanders, then breaks right,
and stops in a big dark scribble-
mess. "What is it?" you ask,
because she won't say,
even though she usually does.

Every word from her mouth
is rain. The picture mist-ifies.
She rises to dance in a pattern
that was the map – you know
now, the picture *was* a map.
Or was it a rain dance step guide?
She's at the messy part,

flopping down on the floor
to scream; but each kick and beat
is rain, rain, rain; the scream
is the hardest you've ever heard
the rain come down. Is there a schematic
for soothing? *Listen*, you tell her
as she pelts, *this is somehow
the strongest sound in the world.*

🏵. Secrets & Schematics

The flattened horizon
level with the frost
crushing sky –

the heart as sound,
do you understand?
& if, last night, I wanted

I wanted for lack
of love, the birds –
not me – wanted the birds,

sparrows unconvinced
but for lack of anyplace else to be.
Here, listen, listen, a cardinal,

the song, listen, listen,
the song is held, safely hidden
behind the magnolia,

& this old girl fallen
wants what, exactly?
The secrets & schematics

of this ruined form poured
when I was born by drunk
machinists who had a lack

of care &
a surplus
of sorrow.

❧ Muck Angel

Our forms are ruined from the first
so that, when we dream of perfection
we move further from the dream.

We are not to blame.
The names we have for what we want –
foremost love –

were wrong at the beginning,
rejoice!
I feel my invisible disability here,

in ruins, some unrealized,
buried beauty assumed broken,
with fear of the construct of utopias.

Daughter, it's my face on the earth,
dirt in my teeth.
Waking up to the rain,

oh love – thank you for making
dirt angels as I slept,
dirt is holier than snow –

🐝 No Muck, No Angel

We are not to blame –
rejoice

in the mistake!

Don't we all dream
our needs are met

& we are cherished?

Unbury
beauty –

ruined & invisible

blue rosebuds
blue rosehips.

Blurred drone

of the workaday world
disowned me

& my child

but beginning is
in every breath

& moment given.

◀ In the mistake is the unrealized

What? Check the mold.
What's called for is null.
And we're the void –

say divine breath,
or happenstance,
regression analysis –

if someone answers
Dream, then bring
me a chamber pot

for the gods to breathe
their breath into –
Cohen and the crack,

Oh god no stop them –
if you answer *correction*,
then you are the employed

technician,
the wise world;
let me hide under the blanket?

♣. Unrealized

What mold?

What void?

What null?

What correction?

Am I in error
again?

All I know is

    dream
    breath
    blankets

Definitional

I run from person to person,
fire to fire,
and say: *We have so little time together.*

No fires are extinguished,
love as sum
undiminished,

oh my little creature,
run from recognition to recognition,
take care in the weeds,

dive through the brambles,
drop a bucket into another fire
at your peril,

live in the rain,
let the rain be your prayer
for the needless.

🌹. Psychotic Symptom or Uncommon Reason

If they come for you
with a microchip
set yourself on fire

I tell my kid
but I mean me
We have so little time

maybe forever
together
in this life & in others

Recognize
extinguished fires
& all creatures

as beings worthy
of love
Love I can't believe

I vomit up this stuff
freely & mean it
who have I

unbecome
by sitting every morning
snow or sun

No one is more surprised
than I to find
dandelions

enchanting
& gold in everyone
ever born

◀ Eyes Open

The ringing on the ground of the vertical trickles, the glug-glug of the gutters, the miniscule strikes of the gong multiply and resonate all at once in a concert without monotony, and not without a certain delicacy
– Francis Ponge

Rain in the backyard, part hitting the garden – yes –

Eyes close.

From inconstant spit to regular patter, then gradations of intensity – to a continuous individuality, tiny waterhammers hitting surfaces asynchronously. Droplets on the roof tile, a low and quiet tap; on window glass, more of a slap; on the walnut leaves, little thwacks; and on the grass, a palatial sibilance. From moment to moment, differentials of volume dependent on amount and wind – a gust creates an overpatterning atop the patter. Sound removes the focality until the wind comes, but then it is gone and we return to the general violent ambience, the dropquakes, and soon the water hits pooled water, making a more absorbed roar as contribution. No, not true – the distracting, malignant sluice of water through the eavestroughs, the busy useful continuous sloooosh above pulling the mind away from the individual fates of drops. The discipline is to ignore the sloosh and try to hear the rain hitting the eaves themselves, and then to return to the void noise.

The glass door, so buffeted by light rain, the best kind – allowing for the most distinctions in timbre, of the individual collective song – rumbles open. On skin:

pre-mist, in the backyard where I feel it fall, the occasional shock of clear spit. Until and if it builds, to rain, quasi-mist, enfolding over the exposed body, handsarmsfaceneck as small immersive coldwet, always this mist in the heaviest rain, the air comprised of rain's self and spirit; overlay of discrete still-sourceable splats until the rain hits a coating of spent rain and the feeling is of meeting, a spreading static wetness, and the mischievous wind comes to differentially impress parts of the body, now working through thin polyester and denim, creating a heaviness to pull against the tactile-board of desensitizing exposed skin, all the thresholds quelled by the impressed saturation, sensory needs settled into the other side of sensation. The body has been rained on.

🦋. Indefinable

I started not broken or flawed
but always part of that creation,

but the manifestation of the language,
its crucible, cried the words

or —

I began broken according
to language, malformation

manifest, my words creating
misery, all flaw, great worm

or —

I began unformed, flawless,
language manifesting because I am

the crucible perfected
sun, moon, darkness & hummingbird

All Flaw

My ruination
is a cistern with a crack,

a heart that thought,

a detail that thought
              itself small,

but was instead part,

it's still the rain!

              The rain

that is the same sound
through the monitor.

I thought
        the perfect sound

was the soothing rain,
but it is also a ruined form

too, a broadcast stillness.

My utopia of rain
lists into a failed state

where the other names
flatten

into a crack up my side,

rainbarrel and echo,

each life an incalculable
drop

I'm focused on,

one precious life,
but I cannot tell which,

     or when,

and have to admit
I'm yet cleansed.

Call it prayer or hatred,

all the other names

     I am cleansed

🖤 Maybe

The rain is songbreath
we are in agreement
& fear

is lack of love
I want to not write
but these hands

don't belong to me.
We almost died
yet here we are & we will die

Maybe we almost die,
every night & each morning
we choose to be alive

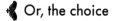 Or, the choice

is soothe, soothe,
rain, rain,
turn the cheek,
feet on the ground
and more rain.

Keep in love,
love, keep
the little ones safe,
safe in their befores,
before we're gone,
gone before dark,
dark coming sooner each day now,
now each day is soothe, soothe,
rain, rain,
my slapped cheek salved wet,
but wet from before,
before the rain,
rain before the soothe,
soothe the pain.

No semantic games –
motion is recursive, just try,
try to get back to the beginning,
beginning with the question,
why –
why –
why –
and the choice is not to not answer,
to not need to answer,
to have rain as answer.

♀. The Buzzard of Artemis

I dare death with every staircase,
every spoonful of bad medicine,

mythical heroines X-ed out
of every hero's journey or cut

down to a footnoted female relative
of little or no significance,

my mother was a mirror
for her sister's pain, I wonder

if I ate mine *in utero,*
"how like a Scorpio,"

every story is America,
American, we don't need

your war machines,
the dusty web of kings

crouched in crashed planes,
we don't need much,

not much is essential,
love, bread, blankets,

medicine baskets,
starlings, grackles.

🦃 Sadness wraps

itself into an ouroborous of consolation,

and I'm shit out or eaten,

a piano ballad making a statement to the world at 3 AM in Times Square,

pavement vomit picked at by drizzle.

Bristle, sound, rain,

a story of three nouns I told my son,

my daughters,

and called it myth

but was just a bid for survival.

The prayer suggests *together*,

and we do, and we are,

rain and rain and rain.

Distraction technique?

Grounding technique (I am on the ground, all flaw, a fallen muck angel)?

Sacred technicians of the wound and not the healing,

tell me –

if I hiss at the wound, will it fester?

Or is the prayer a rewinding of injury?

Little girl with the birds,

and boy of what I know not what will come,

I re-erect the ruins.

My bid for protection spells just an ourobouros of consolation

that finds fire welcome and resurrects fire

with messages of fuel.

Oh, so little time together, and yes, mythic prayer.

Ferocious love, what are you for?

Who?

🖤 An Ouroborous of Consolation

Ferocious love, what are you for? Who?

For self for self no sin
to love self ferociously
& tender   Poet, heal thyself

or keep buying in
to the world's bullshit,
the lie you aren't perfect

You are perfect   You are fine
you were never broken it was a lie
Love requires an honest accounting:

no one is bad, no one isn't
worth saving but there's nothing
to save no need for redemption

Everything that you've done
is because you are human
& everyone

forever praying to not get eaten
in an ouroborous of consolation
& distraction

🦊 Alpha and Omega

We
we are ·
we are nothing –

If I'm scripture, then I'm the kind dictated by mad gods
to madmen as their *Revelations* –

If I am anger and righteousness
then I am the right kind of poison to kill them –
is this is my purpose?

So that we,
we,
can be inconsoled,
unmeaningable,
of no consequence in an obliterated empire,
unkindness kept not as ash or dust,
but between us,
scattered,
dispersed as kindness

❦ Moods Shift With Weather

I have no revelations
some flowers from last year
sprouted, dependent

on the weather I type words
like I care   Do I care
I wish I didn't

it hurts so much less
to not be here. I want
to be

kind a kind of nothing
hurts less & isn't something
anyone can point a finger at

to trust is
too fucking hard,
I can't divine

intention
& wonder
why I bother?

◀ Hephaestus of Fire

The old dream, oldest, of gods:

a blacksmith, who made the weapons of the gods –
a god himself,
of fire and artisans –

Ἀμφιγύεις, *the lame one*
Κυλλοποδίων, *the halting*

With the power of motion
(that persists in me as chaotic movement)

and a clubfoot, exiled from Olympus
for either defending his mother
(I have done this, as a child) from an angry god,
or for being disfigured –

the irony is simple:
the disabled god
makes the tools for the abled gods,
he is their accessibility –

Hephaestus, of fire,
cuckolded by the most beautiful wife, Aphrodite,
his fire stolen by Prometheus and given
to humans –

oh old dream, I'm sorry, I don't dream,
have none,
but waken breathless,
a heaviness on my neck –

🥀 To Walk With Anyone in Any Garden

There is only the song
which is nothing, not green,
unloved, unheroic, ugly

littlesong lost
Consider what was wanted,
walking, to walk with anyone,

what pleasure, what effort
What kind of paradise
praises the golden only,

not the poor, sacrificed
Differently rootless,
an unseen garden shies

from what's perceived
as light   Our bodies are not
beautiful or wanted,

not noticed or desired,
our bodies are only lowly
dandelions, deformed

clovers with lucky
fourth leaves,
three-legged dogs

♚ Who shall wear the robe and crown?

As I went down in the river to pray,
I sang the littlesong you have seen, perhaps heard
in your shelter called body –
the nonsensesong, the brokensong,
the non-song I make of experience and time –

song of a child and a screen
and postictal eternities –

littlesong, my throat constricts as I sing you
so the words come out as gasps,
little irrigative tears –

As I went down to the river to pray,
I had no prayer except collapsing,
seizing, screaming;

I had the dirt, wet at its edge,
I had the littlesong that is the double edge,
I had Hephaestus in mind & praying
to Hephaestus,
praying to fire, for fire,
for the old resolution to conflict
lit by burn – the burn in my throat,
an inability to speak, to say good things,
to heal,
just the screen-moment; a child in my arms,
soon to seize again,
and nothing to be done.

Yes, we are nothing,
nothing   like this

❦ The Crimson Permanent Assurance

I was a desperate seventeen-year-old girl
in dirty bars, wandering the city

to escape home, longing
for a kindness, for a prophecy, to unfurl,

desperately longing to live, to want
to live, to be wanted in the living sea

that is a city & its fabulous citizens
the cold fishes, the coffin hulls

of towers like great ships threatening
the sky, each other in their vastness,

their Kafkaesque enactment
of annihilation, pirating seagulls

for airspace, erasing wilderness
& freedom form by tedious

form, domestic a dirty word
like confessional, earnest, birds

singing their own songs, it's none
of our business what ants do in winter,

to live, to have to live broken
& the parts fall out of place, each song

true to its singer, each singer
the hero of their own song, who can say

what anything means to another,
the sun burns on the ceaseless sea's

songlight as wave after wave after wave

🎵 Broken & the parts fall out of place, each song true to its singer

Anthem: in each is the misalignment,
the golden rule turned to iron bind,
depending; in each the good intention
that excuses the outcome in absence
of recognizing the bind's effect.
We call ourselves good! Oh, we're
the best! And in our goodness
we've followed iron orders. True
to the singer, yes; we must strain
to hear, sometimes, while sounding
the iron ring as warning, letting
the clang scare the very best
out of their reveries. What comes
of our gambits is the truth of matter,
not the why; this, the true song of earth,
and I trust the earth, not the 'best'
among us but the us of dust among us.
If you have a complaint, reader,
do sing it; and if that index finger
isn't pointing, also, right back
at your own heart, then you will
never be rain, just rust in the rain,
close enough to believe in your own
song. The rain is generous,
rain will let you have yourself.

♀. Oh, the shouting, & I am still so afraid

Listen, I am the Fool, listen,
silence is not complicit,

swallows the shout, the should,
the song, the uneven words,

the furious springs of motion,
the inner & outer cores

of stars, there are no laws
or gods we did not craft,

gropingly, from terror.
The word *should* was banned

from the domestic violence
support group, as it implies

another choice when none
is possible, I want & suffer,

what is the even word,
Death in measured tones,

the doctor delivering the news
quietly, unshouted, eye contact

with no heart behind it,
an insulting mask

that says you aren't worth
the effort, it isn't kindness,

the body cannot lie,
love commands nothing,

demands nothing from us,
raise your voice   only in song

I sing the wrongsong, as usual

If silence is complicity,
remember – speech
is law. How did we
get here? Oh, with
the best of intentions
and a committee-approved
SOP. We ruled ourselves
the way we wanted.

> Who outlawed silence?
> Who took my inability
> to speak, to not
> know what to say,
> to question my right
> to utter, and condemned it?

You *abuser*. You
hatemonger. You
courtesan! Fop! Entrepreneur!
You *thief* who would take
my quiet room
and convert it to torture
chamber, echo chamber,

> Hephaestus, come!   Come Hephaestus,
> Hephaestus, come,   come!

In fire! Bring me
the weapon Complicity,
the kind that got you
exiled from Olympus.
Hephaestus, let this
not be the new law.

If you are the forger of weapons,
do not fashion the weapon
that meant your banishment!
It is in the determination of silence
and speech that makes the weapon.

They already have it, Hephaestus!
You need do nothing!
Be silent!

🖤 What I talk about when I talk about love

Trembling under a blanket with no one to tell,
& hoping the next day the pain
will not come again –

Yes, it's getting up again,
this power, the deepest skeleton,
the motion of thing seeking thing

seeking flowers seeking song
seeking the scripture
of a mother's arms,

our mortal wound,
the lovers, us, dead
& rotted,

what we call love riots,
cries vengeance & violence,
right, wrong, righteous,

wrought iron fences,
razed down monuments
where the kids leap forward, again.

I have been an ashtray, a cumrag,
an afterthought, a hashtag, a footnote,
a bathroom scrawl,

love, love,
you love it, you love it,
yeah, suck it, O, baby,

all decisions
have consequences –
the poet says that love informs & governs

❧ Informed government

The motion of thing seeking thing

no seeking a *thing*

nothing

the poet says that love
informs & governs

the poets say nothing true,
not anymore

the unacknowledged legislators of the world
now arbitrate for the acknowledgement
of judges, juries, and elocutioners

love is not information, not really
it is meaning grafted onto emotion
that transforms into the truth

we'll die without

🐛 O Slimy Leaping Heart

O slimy leaping heart that won't
stay down, you stupid motherfucker,
stay down, you are not

a mechanism built with a certain
number of beats in-born,
scheduled to wind down,

you are not a struggling muscle,
fist-sized & furious,
you are not a motor, a stone,

a cog to slot
into the great machine,
you are not a word,

not even a song,
O slimy leaping heart
that is alive,

alive,
alive in violent
loveliness

▉ But I want to be a song?

I want to be a hymn, the wordless kind
that brings to mind a curious feeling
like the wind that unsettles as it comforts,
striking some as wrong and others
as right and the earth as possibly
a signal of rain to come,
oh, I went down to the river to pray,
that kind of hymn that's the accompaniment
(not cure) to pain,
a score. If that is all I could be,
if I could be that.

🌷. To Be Honest With the Earth

In so far as I descend & listen,
in so far as I lie in filthy silence
& self-contempt,

in so far as I descend defeated
by the buzzing maze
of every day,

in so far as I descend bewildered
by the paltry words of gods
& men,

in so far as I descend & consent
to be carried along
by their wandering attentions,

in so far as I descend to be honest
with the earth, living only
in service to song.

❧ Such power you grant your enemies

a doctor once said to me. No more
than they had in the first place?

I'm not burnt out, I'm burnt in.
The devil passes out cigars

and says, *The sloganeer is here.*
The devil means my doctor.

The devil takes care of me, see.
He's a caregiver to the truth too,

the devil can't lie. He makes
deals that are ironclad,

that rust in the rain. *Well,*
their power wasn't granted

by me, I said. *They had it*
all along. The contract was,

I had to love them. Because
they were good. And now

it's wrong of me to still
be in thrall? That's not how

power works, I said. *Or time.*

♥. Imperative

Isn't mockery
a different kind
of love? Screen
becomes shadow
becomes song
becomes sky –
you need
to stay so long
they forget
they feared
your leaving,
so long
they're not
undone
which is
to say
you must
grow old,
singing

◀ Acceptance is the Key

I want to agree. I want that alchemy,
Hephaestus's forge at autonomy:
making the weapons, armor, implements,
an interchangeable world. But the spirit
of mocking returns as unforgettable fire –
the body cursed with assigned shame –
and any agreement I want is dispersed
on the wind. I've burned it in an instant,
with the old fire that comes of its own
accord. That there is a purpose to all
things is so, just so; but that there
is a misapplication as part of purpose is

the part of the purpose

I refuse, and thus am not wise,
not as you; an unbalanced fool,
attempting to place nothing in relation
to purpose.

♥ Unknowing Animal Sorrow

Yes, only suffering,
only pain,

not a rag, torn-off,
fraught with hate,

anticipating hate,
taught to tear ourselves

to tiny pieces
subject to scans

& scopes, screams
cinched-in, negating

the entirety –
sunsets, sickness,

songs, the unknowing
animal sorrow

that holds within it
the whole universe.

🔥 Nothing Pedagogy

Let us be the pedagogists of nothing,
for we are masters of impermanence,
squanderers of days. Self-destruction
is the skyearth's constitution.

Yesterday, a poet wrote me and said,
How do I go on when the world
offers conformity as its only answer?

      I said, *Fire*

(What else? The bible courses with it, cleansing fire)

        I said, *I was born non-neurotypical,*
           thus hated and shunned from birth,
           and learned to either survive
           by asking questions, or agree to die

        I said, *The truth hurts by its nature*
           and no one will thank us
           because this is truth's confirmation,
           the pain of it! that it is not welcomed,

           that the truth must hurt because the truth
           always condemns and kills the
           messenger, too, because the messenger
           is complicit – not silence, but messenger –

He said in response, *Thanks,*
that was much needed

but I felt sadness in being thanked,
at being needed in this way,
based on another null pedagogy:

He that is without sin among you,
let him first cast the stone at her.

May the second and third stones be boomerangs.

The sky commands me, *Look,*
displaying the tools of self-destruction
I equip as the truth –

without argument, perhaps,
but without the will to live too,
for my self-destruction is argument and lack of same.

In lieu I bend, break, and crack,
suggesting the care that should have been,
but wasn't.

In echo, I accuse
as ameliorative.

I refuse the heart, I burn it,
and am so consumed. I create
the conditions where others can be comforted,

I sing the chorus – I am the truth of the chorus,
not the tragic hero, but the hero's echo,
the chiding of what he must learn.

All around us, the detritus, the dying,
my son in my lap,
I don't want to look at the sky

I take nothing single in my heart,
nothing unsinged or unimmolated –
I must burn it first to learn

of its nature, like an alchemist
of carbon to other kinds of carbon,
of nothing purified, to know how

an argument will end as I declare, this, too, as my error.

🌹 Pink From Head to Toe

I fear you all make fun of me but
that's what I get, it's none of my business
what other people think

about anything, I mean,
it's usually nothing,
I would have googled pedagogy

but I learned that word
from a textbook company
when I passed for sort-of able-bodied,

naturally, it didn't last
Thoughtcrimes can't be punished
if we don't care what people think,

I think I read that in Thich Nhat Hanh
or am I lying to get you to meditate
It's just that I love us I mean you

I mean me, I can't believe I preach
what the fuck happened to me?
I wear colour now, pink head to toe,

it makes me feel
what's that word, happy?
Everyone is a brilliant asshole

with an opinion
as fleeting & boring as a revolution
We could be new as morning sun

♥. Heal thyself by healing others as they heal you

Nothing real is verifiable by machine,
nothing real like love & life & what you *feel*.
No one dreams of being conditioned

to be mean, meaning leached from every
interaction, no one means to reproduce
the abuse, no one means to not meet

your eyes when they treat you like a liar,
guarded by popular narrative & financial
incentive, legalese & invective,

evicted from ERs & no, no, no, not intact,
professionalism is an *act*
& what it cost to claw it back,

to keep clawing it back from the rigid
systems, aren't we sick of policing
each other, radically flawed is perfectly

human, no proof needed of pain,
selfsame, selfsame, mess & shame,
medical space is the birthplace

of the fundamental mistake:
we are all different,
we are all the same.

BOOK 3:
Death Record

Jumper

Is this dangerous, should I call Here 24/7,
like I tell my patients? Listening to the same
song, Miley and Noah Cyrus harmonizing
"I Got So High That I Saw Jesus," and I
either need to drink or lay down in the snow.
I think of friends and ask, 'What could I say
that I haven't before?" I don't know. Perhaps
the point is repetition has procedural magic,
transferring pain from hand to hand
as a secret smuggled out of a police state,
warmed at each transfer. But Miley and Noah
feel like water finding the lowest place –
is this low enough? What I need is some
lesser illness, a less authenticating burden.
I shall choose what I see, at the end.
I shall see the void to come: if I told
my wife, again, that I wanted to jump
from the bridge spanning the Niagara
escarpment, with eyes blessedly closed,
then would my heart be lightened
from its task? In the 2003 long past,
poems played patty cake with suicide,
but now I know they are suicide's form –
the process whereby we choose a well-
brewed poison to persevere. The rivers
running dry? At the end of your life,
who better as witness, to say it will all
be okay? I want no one, just the ground
to prove it was always there, that I was water too.

🌷 Here 24/7

You are the ocean, no burden, needed
& seen. I sit in snow & transfer pain
from my right to left & back again,
negligibly, it lessens. Is there a lesson?
No one knows. Listen, the song *is* the secret.
You *are* air & fire, its warmth, & earth feels
the burn of your agony. What could be
more dangerous than the unspoken chance
to know each other's difference & stay
open in witness? Not transference
but common, shared between us, the suspect us.
Some songs ask more from the anomalous.
I won't lie, it won't be okay, this is how
it is. You're already here 24/7. Perfect.

Undertow

This old rhythm of suffering and solace,
of wounds and dressings, then my redress
and wounds again. This body sloshes –
nothing inside me but water that wants
dissipation. I'm no ocean, I'm river –
I'm made

       for pleasure craft and meagre rain.
       For willows and rural, dilapidated pain;
       Bill Bagley's son disappeared,
       but thought to have jumped from Burton
       Bridge; cracked wharves with rusted
       iron hooks; cabled ferries; cows kicking
       tents on the small islands. Crow
       squadrons scouring Transcan garbage;
       churches of two kinds, Catholic
       grands and Protestant modests,
       each installed along the road, all dying.
       The vanished restaurants, I lick
       their red paint. Oh god slap my mouth
       closed, I'll say it: for love.

But love of acreage that needs a drink,
just as its people do – I serve dryness.
So often is service required.

I'm driving down a dirt road impassable
for days after a deluge, now open. Neil
Young's singing about being the ocean.
Fool – a boy from the prairies, what could
he know? But when he makes the rhyme,
"I'm the undertow," I suddenly agree
as sound warbles out of Ford Ranger's
dash. *Yes,* I think. *Lower. Get lower.*

🏵. The Same Waves

Cracked wharves, cabled ferries, towns emptied
but for the churches, squadrons of crows picking
at parishioners poised at the graveside
edge. Poppy carried me to the cemetery
tripping halfway into the hole – nothing
inside me that still doesn't love a bridge
to die from, swung out small over the height,
this body hollowed by the long habit
of fright. The ocean is more than water;
rivers, rain, prairie grasses in wild wind
make the same waves as theta, delta, REM,
this old rhythm, of wounds & dressing,
solace & suffering, protest & pain,
neglected restaurants, children, everything.

Lines that mark the peak and trough

The graveside edge defines
where my shoes sit at night
/ my side of the bed. Sure,
ocean dissolves secrets
of the deep that are metaphors
for life; ocean is how
our rough beast first crawled
on land, desire our ancestor,
but waves are not mine.

They say I fixate on water,
but only as drops that fall.
They say I deserve to live,
that I am good. They told
me to say affirmations
with them. Bless, bless.
I say water is with me in
my sadness. I say that water,
if wave, is waving goodbye.

I'm a line, drawn straight
down; think ballistics,
trajectories of love dropped
from hand to ground, again
and again; of sending toy
boats out to capsize and sink;
of messages in a bottle that say,
I wanted this bottle to never
reach you, to break. Success.

Roxanna, we enact our fates.
Mine? A gaze that knew
its lover as a line, a secret
connect-the-dots of two.
Having broken the connection,
where may I place the pieces?
Oh, with you. An anti-Hallmark
card of a long line that means,
We accelerate as we go.

❦ No Escape

This body hollow becomes a vacuum
that sloshes – nothing inside me but water
that wants to overflow & spill its wet
guts full of empty lobster traps & trawlers,
I want to drink because Steve has cancer
but that's not it, I want to scream & beg
& cry, I wish I could get high but no drug
breaks through the pain, no escape
from the fact that everything dies,
Blow-Me-Down, no one here gets out alive.
Will the ocean wash me clean of wanting,
gentle my dreams, haunted by what-could-
have-beens. Without this sickness,
please don't let him die, could I have made a difference?

The difference we make is already made.
A line demarcates one side.
Categories of like and unlike.
Definitions of worth.
The line has sadness on one side.
Phenomenologically, we draw a line.
They do not believe.
The line is how we fall together.
Would I be without sickness?
The sickness has been with me
In my sadness is a plea to be loved
Straining to be what I cannot –
A hero of mine once shouted love.
I want to die I want to die I want
To be no form, to take no form.
To be free from the line as normal.
If my sign is presignified as difference.
If as I lay my children down to rest.
I have always known, I have always.
That we are going to die is not the problem,

What we aren't is a perfect image.
Division and subdivision refine difference.
Definitions of life and death.
Definitions of lack.
The line has us on the other.
We either believe or do not.
The line is not the difference between you and I.
Without what sickness would I be?
 I've always been with sickness.
in my sadness is my sickness.
from across the line – the perfect image.
– the perfect image is insulated from sickness.
The asylum waits for me to shout.
to be or not to be no doubt or lack.
To have never been born.
To have made my signature.
If the mutter in my wake was a prayer.
If they could be spared the difference.
Run from the enforcers of difference.
the problem is they want us to just go away.

❤ To Be Unwritten Upon

If a poem is ritual or ridicule, still, it helps
as individual strains in a symphony swell
to a soaring – or does it only feed the deluge?
It hurts to feel, I thinned myself as paper
to be unwritten upon, I loved nothing other
than a darkness that could not love me back
because it was empty of all but its own agony,
I am empty of all but my own agony & am nothing
but the lack. Have I not died in lieu of love
a thousand times, loathing the future, its scribes,
all the parables, lies that did not & have never
described how loathsome to be alive.
We don't recover. We become something
other, in time, the song changes, it all changes.

I hate, too. Everything, but mostly me in relation to.

🎐 I am empty of all but my own agony & am nothing

but the lack

and whosoever among us is full; the king who commands

Take ye your fill –

quiver of arrows soon becoming rain,

some may never fill the expectation,

some may stand in the dark and commune with the excavated self;

I'm comfortable nowhere, unalone –

Rain: soothing sound, irrigate the graves

Diagnostically, this word record would indicate the low pole –

Diagnostically, the world is more broken than I

am unfilled –

Window, rain, through the glass I am crossing the line,

am permeable

metaphor lack as less than dark and less than rain,

but the artificial expectation to be more than transfixed

by the excess out the window.

♣. I empty of all

To commune with the excavated self: uncomfortable
everywhere, unalone –

Rain: waves, musculature
undulates

Diagnostically, the world is my deep fake

un fills me –
overflows

rain, through the glass, rivulets running
red roofs, worn grooves

There is no line to cross & we are ever
permeable

Not metaphor, not lack as less than
but actual dark & literally less than

rain, rain, purpling limbs, liatris,
clover, I am transfixed by the excess

of love, its pounding cloudburst,
& I unstable

🌻 The sunflower I remember

lived on the corner, peeking above a suburban fence. If I told you
I was in love, would you believe me? The flower reached for the sun –
a delivery on the provenance of names. Perhaps I shall change
my name to Doomed. My cells reach so too, but I am not beautiful.
Above me now, the sunflower I remember genuflects slightly
at the top, as if it's head couldn't face the sun directly – too much
glare & Icarusity. If I told you I want to die, just let me? Nod yes,
as the world does, as the sunflower I remember does in the wind.
Be the confirmation of a lack of care that prevails from the cradle.
In Oakville, we have the lake effect. Graves author gravity's force.
Twenty years ago, I'd climb the fence when drunk and sleep
at the base of the sunflower I remember, pretending to ride the neck
stem to some messy, imagined heaven. I got drunk too often,
dreamed every day; found heaven, never. Have you ever wanted
to die like a klaxon blares at the end of a factory workday? Oh,
to heave the self effortlessly up to the flowertop. The best thing
about the sunflower I remember is it didn't care about me, yet
was the most lively thing on the street, day or night. This is a life
lesson. I felt it straining to be more alive, every second. I pole-
waltzed with it one evening when the neighbours' house was dark
and the stars in the sky could not compete with glare reflected
from passing headlights. I was mad, yes; but what are you, really,
deep down? I mean, don't go there, you might find the sunflower
I remember, a fieldful, with sorrows to match. Oh, how I would leap
to caress a care I couldn't have. Can't. Nighttime yellow riots
in the retina, a glossy, bright, textured color too high to touch
from the ground. Oh I want to die, right now. So long ago,
the sunflower I remember rent the sky open for three weeks.
Blue, the usual, terrible blue, bird's egg blue with no depth
or substance, dirty clouds scraping stage left. But the sunflower
I remember, affixed like a medal of honour, a boutonnière
to remediate the dreary, dictatorial, ubiquitous, neverending sky –
the screen where my son dies, unceasingly, that scene blocked
as long as I sat under the sunflower I remember. Silent companion,

certain in a natural rhythm, growing in a struggle season. So many want to fix the world, but I want five more minutes under the poor protection of the sunflower I remember; to subsist in the dark with the knowledge that, in five minutes, a passing car would cast a spark above my head. In December at the time of writing, the mirror reveals ravages. Dust. The blank face, one that professes love. The one that's lost its ambivalence, finally, as the final loss. Somewhere, a coin toss. Somewhere else, a seed in the ground dreams of the sun, so it can make good on its name.

🌻 The Beautiful Sad

I lived off an alley & was not beautiful, have never seen a real live sunflower but dead, fields of dead heads spitting seeds. I have never groaned at love but found it everywhere, in every bloody one. If I told you I want to die, just let me? Hold me, the petals wither, crisp, sere, sun burns a rash, nasty, naturally deficient in vitamins A through Z. Silent struggle companion, natural rhythm is seasons, the world unfixed. I want more, protection for the poor, the dark knowledgeable dust. Why be drunk to fence climb, sleep at the feet of flowers? Prescription: dirt naps, dirty feet, filthy tongues. I fell in love at Donlands, Spadina, Bathurst Station, I fell & fell through turnstiles onto subway platforms, onto the possibility of out, out of this I am not a body, I am not a coin toss, ambivalent, definitely heads down, I will not, cannot confirm lack, full as I am with this twisted back then, the Jones 81 might as well have been home, messy with imagined 9-to-5 lives, transfers ground underfoot, second-hand paperbacks for a buck fifty were heaven, I was mad, yes, am mad, yes, will be yes, mad, yes, she said if no one was angry, nothing would change but isn't this poison? Another kind of mad, she said going slowly up the escalator at Yonge Street Station in her purple paisley velvet bellbottoms, the ones with the jewelled hems, you should have seen her, like a garden in a girl, a thousand flowers opening in her face, I would have but it was the 80s you know, so I followed a long-haired boy home instead, he kept a collection of records like a museum curator, what is it we hope to preserve? The note, the song frozen between leaves of glass, pressed wax, a choked throat. I love your sunflower, you climbing fences, drunk with love, I love you, beautiful sad mirror, ravaged by loss.

⚓ Invisible Frequencies

On the bed, at night, I feel the lines.

They say this:

You are good.

The best part of the world is dominant, it wants me to be alive.

I draw an x at the bottom of this rhetoric.

X

Jump.

I'm sorry, there's too much,

sitting still is just me on me, discoursing.

Listen: the quiet things

are trying to save us.

But I'm in lack of letting them.

Spanning the divide of a line

is a bridge I have yet to jump from.

I scratch the line I've just written

and hear the invisible frequency,

a song that goes *Please, no* —

❦. The X

In the closet, at night, I fail to feel
I am good.

The best part of the world is poetry,
the best part of poetry

is you, this
jump into possible, the X.

    I'm sorry
    there's so much

    me, me, me,
    discoursing.

Listen: quiet things
will save us

if we let them,
& this

    my friend
    is the quietest thing

My mother refused to sing, but so did I

Look at the marsh bridge built for my mother.
Dead six years now – I never heard her sing,

not once. Newcastle nuns beat song out of her,
said she had an awful voice. This is why I love

lullabies, having never heard them as a child.
My father got drunk on the back deck listening

to the songs of country music queens, being
lullaby-deficient himself. The only thing he told

of his mother was her saying, "Sit down, shut up,
and pay attention." Am I writing a trauma poem,

entreating you with abuse? Take your leave.
This is about song and how the song stops;

how song was and is confused. Verily: remember
buskers on the streetcorners and at stations who

pay you the kindness of this message: *You are not dead.*
I admit, I'm confused; the song's dragging me down,

coming from below. You're with me, you didn't leave.
Good. You can carry this, like I do. Carry this?

Read the bridge inscription. When I wrote it, years ago,
I thought of a little girl, not accomplishments piled

to the sky. This little girl was told not to sing in class
because her voice was hideous. She gave her life

to others and was loved enough that her service
was commemorated in the little town where she lived.

I will never have a bridge. I only want to jump
from them. I wish there were symbols like this

for her in life, but there weren't – just a furious pace
of work. I sent her my books. She always read them.

Once, she gave me a book of her poetry written
when she was a girl. I never read it. I had the chance

to hear her sing and didn't take it, just like everyone else.
The bridge was built for someone to sing in.

Sing for her else the crickets and highway noise
are her song. As a man, wanting death with fervour,

as if it were my work, furiously committed, I realize
the problem only now. Not that I didn't care to listen,

but that I never sang for, or to, her; without the practise,
how could I notice?

🂱. Green & Sweet

I lost my mind
by the side of the Seine,

dropped pieces
at the Berlin Wall

& couldn't swallow,
needed intravenous

vitamin cocktails
If I tell you this frail body

is killing me
makes me want to die

would you hold me, care for me
or carry me outside,

leave me to die?
I don't want to want

to die
by god it's lonely here

by your side

An imperishable villain will not die today

I don't know what to do today,
but always, this imperative: *Die.*

With thoughts of daughters in my
mind, I need air, more air – how high

up can I get, how many metaphors
are allowed to substitute? Scale.

Scope. Warp. Woof. Dreamscape?
Hypnagogy. Some nights, my son

tells me of Max, a bad guy who talks
in the dark, keeping him from sleep.

I'd strangle Max dead, but Max is in both
our heads – with us in our sadness.

The toddler, long-haired doll in her hand,
sits on a yellow block. A beautiful woman

walks into Pearson airport until – she's
my daughter again? My son lingers

with his boots, struggling to know what
to do with them. His face asks, *How do I make*

these work? My face answers, *Air is both risk*
and rope. Such is disabled time. More image

coordinates, then: a small suburb's treeless
street, centre of a curving road. I can't breathe

again, for God holds my thorax between thumb
and forefinger. *Please Lord do not let me go.*

I know I heard your word the whole time,
the omega command, *Die.* I ask my patients,

Do you have shortness of breath? They too lack
air when word becomes vacuum and your pincers

apply. Oh, I used to ask different questions.
What song? How to be free? Why love? Can

you, too, feel sadness like a sweet suffocation?
In just a few seconds, I'll be dead. A thought

I have, or that I am with – *Die* – sometimes voices
itself past the poem I hold over my head like a plastic bag –

Alack

I write a weary reconnaissance from the world under
the watchful pursestringed eye of the good neoliberal
kings. The fabled bluewater of Sarnia slaps the metal

slivers that demarcate cubits of owned shoreline. A.,
the little one, possesses alphabet letter beach toys,
assembling a nursery Ouija on the rocky beach. The boy

levitates on a trampoline as if for the first loved time
he can move his body without fear of falling. I romanticize,
but have earned the bitter bones for sustenance soup.

His arms perpetually bend. Is there a missing 20 degrees
to be found in the world? Begone, dread biomedical dreams
of cure. Let's market the lack as lack. Wind pummels

the trees and rips their deciduous leaves from lancinating
branches. Oh form and attention, on the page you enliven
the perceptual world but out here, circa Inner Me, I've got

a room. I hideously overflow my self-container, uncertain
of what to see, say, or do, but finding every object somehow
more than I can know. I find the condition exhausting.

Question: what is the poem of no social skills in formal terms?
Not lack of others – interiority is social! – or perception-of-feeling
lack, not motive-beyond-the-self thematic lack, but *as form*?

Whatever that poem is, it won't be a formal lack. Form
is all. (Be with us in our sadness.) *Fake it until you make
it*, they said in the hospital. *Mimesis*, I said back unto them.

No infinite horizon for the poem to pull out towards,
just a dense speck at the centre that occupies allthought,
the vortex my sadness is sucked towards. How many times

this self-assessment: *Abstraction is worth no action,
you addict fuck*? The sunset, circa Canada – Sir John
A's statue pulled down in Montreal, colonialism

had a baby and its head popped off. At the children's
clinic yesterday, the doctor asked: *Does K. feel satiety?*
I pulled a fistful of wrappers from my pocket and said,

*The same way hunger is surrounded by hunger,
the same way punishment, the same way the same
is the same.* K. smiled, knowing satisfaction's regulated

in likemind and pleasure is loving despite red warning lights.
Orange comes now through partial cloud cover, the strands
making less a picture in what they are than in their frame:

long arm, monster fist. The world, in revolution, a lie of love,
has mistaken the start for the end, razing clichés to the ground
for the civic good, a crushed and shaken *Goodness*, a shaken

baby *Goodness* – oh Beachy, you sliver of salvation
for a threatened family, save us – all the bad and systemics
replaced by uploaded monuments of, by, and for destruction.

Why the investment in monuments by nation and anti-nation?
Their mutual argument is what, exactly? That the myths
we disagree on are our common ground? When I first found

my love, I thought her beautiful, and she thought me strange –
yet we came to be with one another in our sadness. A cicada's
in the cottage now, wood's tinnitus. On the beach accessed

by half-rappel, we pass the children down to the shoreline
and play a game of Throw-K's-Sticky-Into-The-Lake.
(How can a lake this vast not be tidal?) Middle-aged women

scavenge for remarkable branches. A man deadlifts
big driftwood logs. J. says either for crafting or birding –
I spell ZAK EVOL I into the sand with plastic Ouija.

How much easier would it have been, as they tell women,
to just smile? (The musculature won't work, connections
unmade? And when falsifying the gesture, a buzzing neural

cicada in the white matter.) K. uses Sticky to make a moat
around A.'s castle. Next to my head later that night, I think
again, *What is the form of lack?* An ancient cross-stitch

on the wall bleats I NEED THEE EVERY HOUR. I too need.
Not a cure but antidote for self. All my addict friends are relapsing,
there's no accountability on Zoom – we say to one another, *Hey,*

it's good to see you – and it is – blowing sad while Bobby injects
the blues into the antecubital vein. Be with us in our sadness.
Minutes ago, orangesky turned penetrant on background blue

past teal and I was happy. Is the pandemic behind us, or is worse
to come? Children on the verandah, what names will come
for you? What will be the worst that you hear? When I say

Be with us, I mean it. I also know I cannot be rid of me.
On the sliver of sandy beach, *Beachy*, A. calls it, I erect
a pup tent and call it Baby Castle. On Beachy, K. finds

a bird skull with intact beak and calls it *Treasure*. I answer
Yes, I'll keep it safe, I will. Waves rise in sinusoidal drawl.
I sight-read them as *You exist on a skimming surface*.

Call this form sadness. Why chastise the spill? I need thee
every hour, lake, your calm body knowing it has exceeded
its form, this poem a remnant voice that remembers broken

pieces. If disinclined to want the best things in life, I'll
formulate axioms of conviction in lieu. I categorize sadness
into small, smaller, and smallest; into an empire of stories

told to children so they can't know of empire. Sing anticipation.
Sing of the battered hand. Sing! But define *encompass*? You
want half-rhymed truth told slant, or the query some utter

as rhetorical but I yell as plea: *You don't want me?* Yes, dear,
its love come calling. Who wrote that nighttime was the worst?
Laying down amidst green, incredible green, is worse. The young

stroll lakeshore, a little girl in hot pink shoes reminding me
that things in this world are alive. Remember what it's like?
Scrolling screens for news from friends who remain true to one

another, love in each of their arms? The virus riots among free
bodies in the protectorate, but I have my room and abandoned
parks; a legacy of throats, doves, and wonder. Strangeness:

the white disease on the oaks, what is it? Ignoble birth –
to forget is the field where the dark things grow. If I want
another word, can I give this poem back for its lack?

I fell in love; this is how all my poems start; but then.
Then I fall in love again. A lonely cottage at the end
of the world, Sky commanding, *Love!*, and I've always

believed Sky because someone lives there, shows me
how I'll lose all the things I love whenever I look.
Doctor says this cinema is Hallucination, but I can't lose

anything else so I don't look. Don't look, keep to the cottage:
rotted planks for a floor, suspended above turquoise. Through
the holes, I see another sky: how other lovers are lost, old tale

of how an old woman at the bottom of the ocean creates
the seas with her tears. I see her down there, my mother.
But then. Then all the mothers in series. Sky shows why

mothers cry as the lake drowns sunk costs. Sky says *There
but for, there but for, there but for,* showing me how love
possesses the possessions despite long and wrong lessons:

hands at throats, at the end of blades, shaping the sandcastles
of internet code – *It's because they don't love us* is the lesson.
It's because they hate us. Stick to the cottage, be with us

in our sadness: gentle slosh around the piles thatch the underside
of a peasant's angel wings. Oh love, with level gaze I ask,
If these are the lessons, then what are the choices? Poems say,

Love, what other choice do you have? But love's what sky
has always shown, what water mourns too. But then. Then
instead of falling in love with the latest lesson,

I stick to the cottage and ask, *What do I know? The decisions
I made, were they good? Did I do right? Was the fight
carried on as my mother advised?* The tight formal structure:

she carried me, but I can't remember. Repeat. Remember
running. Repeat. Running. Repeat. With nothing to fear
except symptoms recorded on charts, I embrace flesh

pathologized in the kingdom of them. I want *Wisdom*
but all I have is advice. See Virginia walking out in
the miscomplected lake, soon to be submerged. See

half-hearted Ahab the Passionate turn all language
towards an awful infinite point on the soul's horizon.
I loved them both, was with them in their sadness.

We consider ourselves seduced, but why are we brought
to sad and angry consolations? Why is suicide like the lake,
like a suddenly dispassionate Ahab drowned post-Moby,

like Virginia's dead-float? Our lungs take on water
when our hearts give out – same way. *What's the point?*
I've asked Siri at midnight. Out the window, to the sky,

I say *You may not take the sad and angry consolations.*
What is it, again, that I must do? So many people seem
to know. After all the heartbreak, nothing's gone. Water

seeks its increase, hillocks and shapes conform to impacted
ploughscapes – but carry on? So I do, at night when I can't see
water, when the window seems higher than it should. All these

years, what other testimony? I see water's hint in silent dancing
silhouettes. If I said, *I'm dying*, wouldn't you agree? Image
of two little girls, a boy, a woman indifferent to windows,

a few books on shelves. Logic's for fools who need their dreams
explained. I'm repeating myself, from a book I once wrote.
We repeat ourselves in the end as a reminder to die. In life,

there is pain and a stranger pain (repeating myself again)
called healing that lets windows wait in place. So look
and tell me nothing's gone. Nothing is? Really? The grotesque

lake whispers *Paranoia, psychosis*; and for all anyone
would know, the limitless day keeps saying, *Move on,
like I do*. Take away sadness, and what's left? A boy, is all;

scared, alone, all there ever was – take the briefcase from the ghost,
get to work. Metaphors of protection enfold within metaphors
of threat to fold again. New bodies of the earth: throw arms wide

while falling. Each birth sows arms to open wide, wide. No trick
in arms not holding a thing, a half circle shot out in a startle,
the helpless cradle of the idea of a child in the infant's lay-you-down.

The grasp reflex is held in metaphors of threat, counter to the morrow.
Tomorrow, another threat. Today, another. Descent, arms open wide,
a wide descent. Strange child to the parent, I hurtle out hands to catch

the fear that's placeless, an everywhere grasped as *poor baby,*
                                        poor baby,
            set you down gentle,

                        gently.

🐝. Alas

Poor baby,

                                        poor baby,
            set you down gentle,

                                gently
                    in the cradle
                        in the grave hill

                of sky
                of rain
                of love

Invisible before you were born & again after you die,
in between   we get a life
            Descend, open wide

Medicine is sick,
each birth sows seeds & all depends
on origins   arising

*

I say as though I know
    all of my life
but what do I *know?*

Not think, dirty trick
of the intellect
    but *know.*

I was carried, have carried,
been a carrier of the varied
    consolations

    a veritable
galactic federation
of misplaced love

overflowing my container.
Refrain, the munx say, refrain
    but sustain

the endless hunger.
What's satiety, what's sane?

That no one stays

is plain

*

but that's the nature
    of the game
no one wins or loses

(there is no game).
    Metaphor is all
we ever were

rowing a toy boat
    further & further
from the shore.

I tap-danced across
the cracked backs
    of mussels

at the Bay of Islands
marina while the wind
    made an ocarina

of the quarries
& the caves.
    No one stays,

*

When I first met
      my love
I'd just been raped,

was in an altered state.
      He's patient,
waits & waits

I come away
      from
ghosts towns

without graves,
      oil tanks
that rust into the waves.

Reverend,
      who asked
if I was saved

when I so badly
      needed
to be saved,

Deliver us from love
& all the evil
      it has done

🦋 Be With Us In Our Sadness

Out the window, the same view:
not lack of me, but a container
to fill with attention, with me.

Oh, the time my daughter told me
of a classmate who walked up
to her and asked, *Will you be
my friend?* Of course,
we cannot be friends with
the guileless, we would
share their discomfort and be
with them in their sadness.

If I told you another story
of friendlessness, would you care?
My own, so you can know
me better? We have a secret,
I know it's true, not of love or grief,
but of sitting and dying
section by section, lights going out
in our bodies and the chances
decreasing that the window
will be with us in our sadness.

Desperate, afraid to look one
morning, like I am now with you,
I whispered to Window,
Will you be my friend?

If you've never been this low,
then I can't help you; you can't
be with me in my sadness.

Out the window, no people;
only form, function, and the end.
I could run down the street
and scream *Be with me*, but know
no one would; I could
whisper it to my children,
but they'd be afraid. If I confessed
to my wife, then the hospital
would consume my sadness.

Be with me. Be with me. Oh, love!
I hate this need that has become
pack-muleish; and I can't carry yours,
not anymore. I was with you
in your sadness until my own made
you think, *It's like he needs me*
more than his sadness,
as if he wants to trade it for love
and no, I can't be that kind of friend.

🦋. Birds of Prey

What kind of friend,
what kind of kind –
to be large enough to hold

your pain, the sky
outside the window,
day & night, the lights

winking in my body,
torquing sprites.
Stay gold. Pony Boy

grew old. *Will you
be my friend?*
This forking river

never ends. Will you
give me succour,
still my raging limbs?

I beg reflections to forgive me,
have not felt an answer.
Have you been this low,

so low the mirror
sent you to bed
without supper?

Where are you, is this heaven
or a raging conflagration?
Be my sibling in this

unmeaningless incarnation,
now that I'm slow, so slow,
a pack mule carrying

done days up, always uphill,
love, drag me to the mountain
top & leave me for the birds,

the beautiful birds of prey.
I pray you will be my friend.
I know I'm strange

& so far away you can't depend
but I'm here, out here
& I will always be your friend.

Notes and Acknowledgements

Roxanna:

Thank you Shane Neilson for sharing your poetry.

Thank you Jim Johnstone for the laborious task of editing this Beast.

Thank you Steve Jelliman & Connor Bennett for keeping me alive.

Shane:

Thank you Roxanna, Janet, Zee, Aria, Kaz.

Poems from my contribution in this manuscript were published in *Contemporary Verse 2*, *The Fiddlehead*, *The Literary Review of Canada*, *Vallum*, *The Antigonish Review*, and *The Manhattan Review*.

"Dunce" won a prize in *Stone of Madness* (US)'s 2022 competition.

"Be With Us In Our Sadness" was published as a limited broadsheet by Anstruther Press in 2021.

About the Authors

♥. Roxanna Bennett is a multiply-disabled unbinaried entity living under the sky.

🕯 Shane Neilson is a mad/non-neurotypical poet, physician, and critic whose heart is in New Brunswick and whose clinic is in Guelph.